RELIGION AND CULTURE SERIES

Joseph Husslein, S.J., Ph.D., General Editor

THE QUALITY OF MERCY

THE QUALITY OF MERCY

Thoughts on the Works of Mercy

The Rt. Rev. Hugh F. Blunt, LL.D.

Author of *Life With the Holy Ghost, The New Song,* etc.

THE BRUCE PUBLISHING COMPANY
MILWAUKEE

Nihil obstat: RT. REV. EDWARD G. MURRAY, Censor librorum
Imprimatur: ✠ RICHARD J. CUSHING, Archbishop of Boston
January 9, 1945

The parts of the text of the New Testament contained
in this book are taken from "The New Testament of
Our Lord and Saviour Jesus Christ — a Revision of the
Challoner-Rheims Version," by permission of the Confraternity of Christian Doctrine, Washington, D. C.

Copyright, 1945
The Bruce Publishing Company
Milwaukee

TO
OUR LADY
— MOTHER OF MERCY

Preface

FATHER BLUNT has once more put us under obligation by answering to a major need of our day. Here at last is a book dealing sympathetically and understandingly with the history and practice of the corporal and spiritual works of mercy, as conditioned by our modern civilization. It is the first book, so far as we know, devoted exclusively to this one subject.

For the exercise of Christian charity we can, of course, find no greater stimulus than our Lord's own declaration that what we do for our neighbor in his need we do for Him. It is the love of God as our motive which constitutes that heavenly alchemy whereby can be turned into gold all man's lowliest deeds.

Imprinted unforgettably upon our souls is that dramatic scene of the Last Judgment when, we are told, the Son of man shall come in all His majesty, and all the angels with Him. "Then," continues the Sacred Text, "shall he sit upon the seat of his Majesty, and all nations shall be gathered together before him, and he shall separate them one from another, as the shepherd separateth the sheep from the goats."

Now, in an illustration of such a nature it is important to be specific, and so, out of all possible virtues and their contraries, a single one is selected to drive home the lesson to be conveyed. This then becomes the only test actually mentioned by which Christ, as King and Judge, "shall set the sheep at his right hand, but the goats on his left."

And which, we might well marvel, out of all the golden

registry of virtues in the court of heaven, would be the one singled out by our Lord as justifying in itself this eternal separation of the saved from the lost?

It is no other, as we know, than the practice of works of charity. "For I was hungry, and you gave me to eat," He shall say to the blessed of the Father. "I was thirsty, and you gave me to drink; I was a stranger, and you took me in; naked, and you covered me; sick, and you visited me; I was in prison, and you came to me."

And to their bewildered question — When did they do all this for Him? — He replies with a solemn protestation that in the past has filled the world with institutions of mercy, and has given incentive to a million times a million acts of mercy, and that still shall continue to go ringing down the ages: "Amen I say to you, as long as you did it to one of these my least brethren, you did it to me" (Matt. 15:31-46).

No better recommendation, therefore, could be given for the importance of the subject here treated than the argument deduced from Christ's own words.

It is not that no other virtues are sacred in the eyes of God than those mentioned here, or that no other sins are heinous than the neglect of works of mercy in situations where this can become a serious sin, as the author well explains. Rather it is that in His infinite compassion Christ deemed it sufficient to single out for His tremendous scene of the Last Judgment only the humble works of true Christian charity. He wished that by this virtue His disciples should be especially recognized; and so in every age and every land have God's saints been conspicuous for their acts of charity.

Surely, then, the importance of this book, at the present crucial moment in particular, cannot be overestimated. Father Blunt, in the absence of any other complete work upon the subject, has searched all sources and turned in all directions wherever he might discover and select his material for this comprehensive work. Priests and teachers of religion will find it invaluable; but it is by no means intended only for them. It is for all men and women who on the last day will be included in that great assize and who shall have to give to God an account of their stewardship. They will find it popular, interesting, and convincing.

JOSEPH HUSSLEIN, S.J., PH.D.
General Editor, Religion and Culture Series

Saint Louis University
September 19, 1944

Author's Foreword

IT IS presumptuous to write a book on mercy. It is a *tour de force,* like engraving the *Pater Noster* on the head of a pin, or copying the entire Bible on a postage stamp. For to treat of mercy half adequately would be to give the history of God's dealings with creation from the beginning throughout all eternity; for all theology, all philosophy, all life, is but the history of love. And what is love but the motor of mercy, and what is mercy but the manifestation of love?

But God will pardon the presumption of trying to confine His infinite love within these random thoughts on the works of mercy, which are in truth the very life of the Church. It is the attempt to tell "the little lesson of love," which the Church is forever repeating in the words of our Lord Himself: "Be ye therefore merciful, as your Father also is merciful" (Luke 6:36).

> The quality of mercy is not strain'd,
> It droppeth as the gentle rain from heaven
> Upon the place beneath: it is twice blest;
> It blesseth him that gives, and him that takes:
> 'Tis mightiest in the mightiest: it becomes
> The throned monarch better than his crown;
> His sceptre shows the force of temporal power,
> The attribute to awe and majesty,
> Wherein doth sit the fear and dread of Kings;
> But mercy is above this sceptred sway;
> It is enthroned in the hearts of Kings,
> It is an attribute to God Himself;
> And earthly power doth then show likest God's
> When mercy seasons justice. Therefore, Jew,

Though justice be thy plea, consider this,
That, in the course of justice, none of us
Should see salvation: we do pray for mercy;
And that same prayer doth teach us all to render
The deeds of mercy.

— *The Merchant of Venice*. Act iv, sc. 1.

Contents

CONTENTS

THE QUALITY OF MERCY

HISTORIC BACKGROUNDS

Chapter I

The Bedrock of Charity

WHAT miserable beings we should be without charity! If God did not love us, or if we did not love God; if we did not love our neighbor, or if our neighbor did not love us; if we were just left to ourselves, centered wholly in ourselves, we should be like so many animals — nothing more. Love saves us, where brute force would destroy us. The "survival of the fittest" is the most inhuman of philosophies. Love is not only the center of life; love is the *all* of life. Love alone rules the world.

Our consideration of love in regard to the works of mercy is necessarily limited. Love, or charity, is infinitely broad. Its primary object is God. It is in this sense that St. Paul says: "The greatest of these is charity."

Our chief concern here is with the secondary object of charity — namely ourselves and our neighbor. The ordinary, popular meaning which current speech gives to charity is love for neighbor. That is fundamental. Hence, before considering almsgiving, or mercy — they are the same word in Greek — it is necessary to get down to this bedrock of charity. St. Thomas shows that the perfection of the spiritual life consists essentially in charity. Charity is the stone foundation, and mercy is the superstructure. Or, to change the figure, charity is the root, and mercy is the fruit-bearing tree.

The words "charity" and "alms" are too often confused.
Now charity is not necessarily related to the giving of alms,
since it is much more than that. Charity, not mercy, is the
greatest virtue. For instance, you can conceive of the situ-
ation where everybody in the world would be so rich that
no one needed alms, or on the other hand so very poor
that no one could afford to give alms; and yet, in spite of
that equality of wealth or poverty, there would still remain
the obligation of charity. Almsgiving, therefore, is but
one result of charity. For this reason alms is defined as
an act of charity, the effect of mercy intervening. By no
means is it the *all* of charity.

Charity to one's neighbor belongs to the very essence
of religion. One day a Pharisee, a Doctor of the Law,
asked our Lord this question — "Master, which is the
greatest commandment in the Law?" And Jesus said to
him, " 'Thou shalt love the Lord thy God with thy whole
heart, and with thy whole soul, and with thy whole mind'
(Deut. 6:5). This is the greatest and the first commandment. And the second is like to this: 'Thou shalt love thy
neighbor as thyself' (Lev. 19:18). On these two commandments dependeth the whole Law and the Prophets" (Matt.
22:25). But the commandment to love our neighbor as
ourselves is not a new pronouncement discoverable only
in Christianity. It precedes Christianity, precedes even the
Mosaic Law. It is, indeed, even a natural precept, since all
men are brothers, of the same origin, governed by the
same laws, destined for the same sorrows, the same joys,
the same hopes, the same eternal rest, the same union
with God.

Ordinarily the Christian can learn little from paganism.
Sometimes, however, pagan concepts can be used to point
the natural law. So in regard to fraternal charity. Even
the pagan Seneca declared: "Men ought to regard themselves as being all members of one great body, nature
having drawn them from the same source, and by that

made them relatives one of the other." It is in line with the well-known saying of Terence: "I am a man; I consider nothing human as foreign to me." Alexander Severus thought so much of the Golden Rule, "Do not do to anyone what you would not wish done to yourself," that he ordered the words to be inscribed on the wall of every one of his palaces and public buildings. Very similar was the maxim of the Seven Wise Men of Greece: "Be pleasing to all; hate violence; hate contention; envy no one; be affable; give yourself to all; follow concord; give with generosity." Epictetus makes a plea almost Franciscan in its opposition to riches: "No one who is a lover of riches, or a lover of pleasure, or a lover of glory, can be at the same time a lover of men." And Plato gets very close to the Christian concept of love. He says: "All the sacrifices and the things over which sacred sciences presided, and by which the Divinity unites himself with men, had nothing else for their object but the maintenance of love and its application as a remedy."

High words, but logical for these pagan thinkers. Yet it would be a mistake to regard them as typical, or practical, as we shall see later. Still the truth is that our very reason assures us of the necessity of brotherly love, if for nothing else but the preservation of the race. Otherwise the world and society would be in confusion; nay, more, mankind with its boasted complex of "survival of the fittest" would have disappeared ages ago. Not one child would be born, were it not for the radiating influence of love. Man is a social being. Often he is weak and in need of help, often filled with misery, sick in body and soul. And who, in the Providence of God, is to help him but his fellow man? In such cases of distress he needs mercy, alms, love. Yet, prescinding from all that acute and temporary distress, even if he enjoyed all that his heart craves on this earth, he would still require the love from his neighbor, and, more, the power, the opportunity to give out his own love. Man does not live by bread alone. He finds the most necessary vitamins in love. The dregs of mere animal life will never quench the thirst. To quote Shakespeare:

> I had rather be a dog, and bay the moon
> Than such a Roman.

We do not minimize the fact that love of neighbor is a natural obligation. Nature belongs to the Creator. But beyond that this love has been commanded, glorified by religion. The spirit of religion is the spirit of God and the spirit of God is the spirit of love. "God is Love."

There is a tendency sometimes to minimize the Old Testament, to ignore it, to regard it as entirely superseded by the New. But remember always that the Old Testament, too, is the word of God. And God never changes. Now in the Old Testament there is, from the first page to the last, the unvarying command to love our neighbor, the repetition, or the particular enlargement, or the concrete example, of the precept in Leviticus (19:18): "Thou shalt love thy friend as thyself"; although even here the command seems to have been popularly understood to refer only to a love of Jew for Jew. Yet there are no fewer than three hundred passages, some of them running to many verses, where charity is commanded or praised, besides the narration of beautiful examples of charitable deeds. The Psalms, for instance, have forty-four such passages; Proverbs, forty-nine; and Ecclesiasticus, forty-three. The whole theme of the Book of Tobias is the blessing which God showers upon the charitable. But — and it is a big "But" — as much as the Old Testament insists upon the love for neighbor, it would be a great mistake to judge the Jews, in the time of Christ for instance, as understanding these commands in the sense in which Christ taught universal charity for all mankind. As is evident from the Gospels and other sources, influential sections among the Jews had actually made void the Law by their false traditions. In the matter of charity, the necessity of keeping aloof from the pagans in order to protect their own faith had ended finally in their simply despising all other nations as idolaters, to whom no aid was to be given. They even considered the Gentile infant unclean. The *Mishnah,* an explanation of the Law, forbade aid to be given to its mother, lest the child be brought up in idolatry. In brief, the Jews of the time, under the separatist teaching of the Pharisees, despised the Gentiles, considering them unclean, and as communicating their uncleanness to others, imputed the vilest crimes to them, would not eat with them, would not enter their houses — in a word would have no intercourse with them except in business. For an example, the very touch of a heathen polluted a whole cask of wine.

Contrast such an attitude with the command of Jesus — "Love your enemies." Now this is not to say that the Jew was not charitable. Far from it. He was then, as now, eminently charitable. There was no bound to the liberality of the rich, who, for instance, spent fortunes upon the promotion of Jewish learning. They were openhanded to the poor, unlimited in their hospitality, and they exercised their charity in all delicacy so as not to offend the sensibilities of the needy, even going so far as to provide for the necessary Temple sacrifices lest the poor would experience shame from their inability. Bethesda, for example, means, House of Charity. The Rabbis told the people that to show hospitality to a fellow Jew was as meritorious as to receive God Himself. The popular classes regarded one another as members of the same family and gave help to one another. Yet, as far as we can discover, there was no organized system of relief such as is common today. All in all it was a pretty close corporation. No non-Jew need apply.

Yet there were some fine qualities about the social and

economic life of the time, qualities that affected charity. Take the matter of work, for instance. The lack of wealth did not mean inferiority, consequently there was no looking down on the laborer, for with rich and poor alike a trade was considered almost a religious duty. In the Talmud the chief doctors urged manual labor. "Labor," said they, "is lofty, for it reanimates its master, that is, the man who engages in it." Again, they said, "What a value labor has in God's eyes!" Even the Rabbis worked. It is a striking thing, this dignity of work, in a time of great luxury and consequent moral corruption. We need but compare the Grecian influence with the survival of much real piety among the Jews.

Jerusalem, with a standing population of upwards of a quarter of a million, not to mention the innumerable casual pilgrims and travelers, had much wealth and luxury on the one hand, and no little poverty on the other. But it was hardly a degraded poverty, even though at times there was much destitution, for the cost of living was cheap, meat, for instance, costing only a penny a pound. Life was simple, and wants were few. Corn and wine were abundant in Galilee and the cost of living there was about one fifth of what it was in Judea. Yet life was far from being rosy. There was much suffering among the lower classes. One cause of the poverty was heavy taxation. There were crushing taxes of every kind. The Mosaic Law which had aimed to relieve distress had fallen into disuse long before. There was work enough. The Temple was rebuilding, and nearly twenty-thousand laborers, architects, masons, weavers, stonecutters, etc., were employed. Family life everywhere was healthy, and the children received every possible care, being taught both by father and mother. The great Rabbis were respected almost to adoration. So that all in all social life in the time of our Lord seemed prosperous, even luxurious, absolutely secure; but in truth it was headed for destruction, for too often there was no real charity in it, and without charity, which is life, there can be but death.

There was no foundation; there could be no superstructure. In nothing is that more evident than in the attitude of the religious leaders to the sick and poor. The Scribes disdained the poor and humble. Even to such a leader as Hillel is ascribed the saying: "No man without education can escape evil doing; no man of the common people has ever attained unto piety!" What smug complacency!

If the lot of the unfortunate was bad among the Jews, it was indescribably worse among the pagans, who never had even the remnants of the brotherly love commanded in the Old Testament. Take Rome, for instance. St. Augustine says: "The estate of Rome was never any true Commonwealth, because it never was guided by true justice." He says further, in *The City of God*, "The pagans do not respect goodness, or the integrity of the Commonwealth, they only care that it be rich and victorious. 'Let the poor,' they say, 'obey the rich for their bellies' sakes: and that they may live at ease under their protections; let the rich abuse the poor in their huge attendance, and have them ministering to their sumptuousness.'" Of the population of Rome, two millions — more than half — was slave, with no legal rights whatever. Consequently it was a mass of cruelty and oppression. There was no pity there. Might was right. There was no systematic care of the sick and the poor; there were no hospitals worthy of the name; unwelcome children were neglected. Thus — and it was the same in Greece — the poor were treated with contempt. Indeed, a man was important only as a citizen. As a person he had no inherent value. Hence there was no real sympathy, because there was no tie of humanity, no fraternal love. Human ills were regarded with a stoic indifference, and if at times the government provided help, it was merely a political move, not an effort to aid the poor as poor, since they were not citizens and hence were outside the pale of help. It was the evil of counting polls and not souls. It was a charity — if you could call it charity — far below that of the Jews.

And then suddenly there sounded from pole to pole the clarion call of Christ: "Blessed are the poor in spirit for theirs is the Kingdom of Heaven. Blessed are the merciful, for they shall obtain mercy."

It was not the setting aside of the Old Law. Christ did not abrogate the Law and the Prophets. He came, as He said, not to destroy but to fulfill, to raise the Old Law to perfection, to the ideal willed by God. For, as we have said, it must not be forgotten that the Old Law was the word of God, the true, if incomplete, expression of the will of God. Christ was to etch it more clearly, to sanctify the Law more and more. His was to be a fuller, more perfect evolution of the Law, really a transfiguration of it. As Father Filion says — "Thanks to Him, the Old Law still exists and exercises its full power in the Christian Church, but in a final, supereminent form, as our risen body will be distinct from our mortal body, while not ceasing to be identical with it."

And again: "Jesus transformed and transfigured the Jewish moral teaching, supplementing it by new and more perfect precepts, and by drawing His Disciples' attention to the spirit and import of the Divine commandments, since previously attention had been directed too much to the mere letter, as the Scribes had been satisfied with insisting on external obedience." Christ's transformation of Jewish moral teaching is particularly evident in His teaching as to the filial relations of man to God, of which the "Our Father" is the sublime expression. It is beyond our scope to consider the transforming glory of His teaching about the innumerable truths of religion. We are interested here primarily in His teaching about brotherly love, which, contrary to the Jewish practice of His day, was to include all mankind.

Edersheim says somewhere that, "there is much in Jewish writings and life — the outcome of Old Testament training — that is noblest and most touching, especially as regards the social virtues, such as purity, kindness, and charity, and the acknowledgment of God in sufferings, as well as their patient endurance"; yet Jesus, he holds, was, "alike in the fundamental direction of His teaching and work, and in its details, antithetic to the Synagogue in its doctrine, practice, and expectancies." It was the current perversions, such as those of the Pharisees, to which He was antithetic.

In bidding His disciples to love one another as He loved them, Christ gave what was indeed a *new* Commandment — "A new commandment I give to you, that you love one another: that as I have loved you, you also love one another. By this will all men know that you are my disciples, if you have love for one another" (John 13:34–35). "As I have loved you." Here was the tremendous glorification of charity, the command given to His disciples to love one another as He loved them. It is almost incredible. But you will not understand Christian mercy, unless you grasp that sublime truth of the importance of man in the mind of God.

To quote the sayings of our Lord as to the necessity of loving our neighbor, including our enemies; to enumerate His deeds of kindness, His miracles for the unfortunate, would be to repeat the Gospels almost in their entirety. The texts that command charity or that narrate His numberless acts of love and mercy count up to at least one hundred and fifty.

But that charity did not end with Him. His Divine example bore abundant fruit in the lives of His followers. As Lecky says: "Christianity for the first time made charity a rudimentary virtue, giving it a leading place in the

moral type, and in the exhortation of its teachers. Besides
its general influence, in stimulating the affections, it
effected a complete revolution in this sphere by regarding
the poor as the special representatives of the Christian
Founder, and thus making the love of Christ rather than
the love of man the principle of charity. . . . A vast organization of Charity, presided over by bishops, and actually directed by the Deacons, soon ramified over Christendom, till the bond of charity became the bond of
unity, and the most distant sections of the Christian
Church corresponded by the interchange of mercy."

And this surge of charity, after the teaching of Christ,
is especially evident in the era of the apostles. It was par
excellence the age of brotherly love. It would be next to
impossible to note all the texts in the Acts, the Epistles,
and the Apocalypse, on this subject. They are innumerable. St. Paul, for instance, goes infinitely beyond the Jewish conception of love of neighbor. To him there is no
distinction between Jew and Gentile, barbarian and Scyth-
ian, bond and free. "Christ is all, and in all" (Col. 3:11).
Charity includes even those who are not Christians (Rom.
12:14). What an advance for the formerly Pharisaic Saul!

But it is in the Epistles of St. John that the new Commandment of Christian love is especially inculcated. It
may be burdensome to read a series of texts, but these are
so important that they must be detailed.

"If we love one another," he says, "God abides in us
and his love is perfected in us. . . . If anyone says, 'I love
God,' and hates his brother, he is a liar. For how can he
who does not love his brother, whom he sees, love God
whom he does not see. And this commandment we have
from him, that he who loves God should love his Brother
also" (1 John 4:12, 19–21). "Beloved, let us love one another, for love is from God. And everyone who loves is
born of God, and knows God. He who does not love does
not know God, for God is love" (1 John 4:7, 1–8).

"And this is his commandment, that we should believe in the name of his Son, Jesus Christ, and love one another even as he gave us commandment" (1 John 3:23).

"Whoever is not just is not of God, nor is he just who does not love his brother. For this is the message that you have heard from the beginning that we should love one another" (1 John 3:11–12).

"He who says that he is in the light and hates his brother, is in the darkness still. He who loves his brother abides in the light, and for him there is no stumbling. But he who hates his brother is in the darkness, and walks in the darkness, and he does not know whither he goes; because the darkness has blinded his eyes" (1 John 2:9–11).

"Not as writing to thee a new commandment, but that which we have had from the beginning, that we love one another" (2 John 5).

It is said that when St. John was an old man, his perpetual exhortation was, "Little children, love one another." When he was asked why he repeated that message so often, he replied, "Because it is the great Commandment of the Law, and if one fulfills this, it is enough."

St. Catherine of Siena made that teaching the secret of her sanctity. The Lord said to her: "The soul that loves me in truth also loves her neighbor, and when she does not love her neighbor, her love is not true. For, love of Me and love of one's neighbor is one and the same thing, and so much as a soul loves Me, so much more will she love her neighbor." Again He said to her, "Every virtue is obtained by means of thy neighbor, and likewise every defect: he, therefore, who stands in hatred of Me does an injury to his neighbor, and to himself, who is his own chief neighbor, and this injury is both general and particular. It is general because you are obliged to love your neighbor as yourself, and, loving him, you ought to help him spiritually with prayer, counseling him with words,

and assisting him spiritually and temporally, according to
the need in which he may be, at least with your good will,
if you have nothing else." St. Catherine's whole teaching
was that we can express love of God in love for our neighbor. She was a good theologian. It is what all the Fathers
have taught. To quote a few samples from innumerable
passages. St. Gregory Nazianzen says: "With Christians the
law and rule of friendship is always this: to wish the same
things to neighbors as to oneself." St. John Chrysostom
has it: "The command of the love of neighbor is like the
command of Divine Love." St. Augustine could be
quoted endlessly. "The love of neighbor," he says, "is a
sure step to the love of God." "Every man is man's neighbor." "In charity the poor man is rich; without charity
every rich man is poor." "Ask yourself what progress you
have made in charity, and according to the answer of your
heart you may estimate the measure of your approach to
heaven."

Love of God, and love of all men on account of God —
there is the root of spiritual growth. All the works of
mercy are the flowering of that. St. Gregory has that
thought: "Our Lord's precepts are many, yet only one;
many by diversity of work, and only one in the root of
love." An old spiritual writer, Blessed Oelred of Rivaux,
puts it very strikingly: "What is temperance but love
which no pleasure seduceth? What is prudence, but love,
which no error enticeth? What is fortitude, but love,
which endureth adverse things with courage? What is justice but love, which composeth, by a certain charm, the
inequalities of this life? What, in short, is the whole of
Catholic religion but a certain little lesson of love?"

So the Middle Ages were ages of love as well as ages of
faith. "Love," writes Digby, "was glorified in the human
intelligence, and recognized as the only remedy for the
woes of the human race." Love was everything. "Beg our
Lord to grant you perfect love for your neighbor," says St.

Teresa, "and leave the rest to Him." She always had that charity. She says of one of her nuns, "Her love of her neighbor was very great, for she used to say that she would resign herself to be cut into a thousand pieces for anyone on the condition that he did not lose his soul." So, charity, in the sense of love of neighbor for the love of God is the bedrock of life.

Again, it is the root, bursting into the bush that blossoms into flowers of mercy, the Burning Bush, that is thereby filled with the Presence of God. It is, indeed, our "little lesson of love," a little Kindergarten primer now, but laying the foundation for our increasing education in love until the blessed day when we will abide in Love and become united with the God of Love.

Chapter II

The Gospel Command of Alms

ST. AMBROSE says, "Where there is perfect charity, there is all faith." Charity is the solid foundation of life. You do not really love God if you do not love your neighbor. All men are brothers because they are children of God. He is the Father of all, the real owner of all goods, and man only His steward. Love of neighbor is absolutely essential, even though, as we have seen, conditions might be such that it would be impossible or unnecessary to give alms. In nothing is there so much loose thinking as in the obligation of loving one's neighbor. So many people mix up love and affection. They have real affection for certain people, as for the members of their own family. They can grasp that. But, they say: There are a lot of people for whom I feel no affection whatsoever; this, even for people I know, let alone the hundreds of millions whom I shall never know; yet, I am commanded to love all men, even my enemies — how can I have affection for them? The answer is that you do not need to feel affection for them.

I know of no one who put this matter as clearly as St. Bernard, in his book on "The Love of God." He distinguishes between charity in action and charity in affection, and asks how could charity be imposed upon us as an obligation which could in no wise be attained. He says: "That the commandment applies rather to charity of action appears perfectly clear from the fact that when the Lord had said, *Love your enemies,* He immediately added concerning actions, *do good to them that hate you.* In similar strain the Old Testament says: *if thy enemy be hungry, give him to eat: if he be thirsty, give him water to drink.* And here, you see, there is reference to action, not affection." Of course, he adds, that even in charity of action there is a certain amount of charity of affection. So that this charity of action, benevolence, or beneficence, or alms, is not a virtue distinct from charity, but is a certain special act or effect of it, though some theologians call it a special virtue, distinguishable from charity, though a product of it. Some scholastics refer it even to justice. Hence while you may feel no special affection for your neighbor, you are bound to love him, by wishing him well and by helping him in his need, if you are able to do so. It has little to do with any special friendship; it is broader than that. It is the very part of the life of sanctification. It is a striking thing that in Hebrew the word "holy" means also "mercy."

St. Thomas puts it succinctly: "As love of our neighbor is a matter of precept, whatever is a necessary condition to the love of our neighbor is a matter of precept also. Now the love of our neighbor requires that not only should we be our neighbor's well-wishers, but also his well-doers, according to 1 John 3:18, 'Let us not love in word, nor in tongue, but in deed and in truth.' Now, in order to be a person's well-wisher and well-doer, we ought to succor his needs, and this is done by alms-giving. Therefore alms-giving is a matter of precept." This alms-giving is defined as an act of charity, the effect of mercy intervening. What a beautiful definition St. Thomas gives of mercy: "a heart suffering over the sufferings of others." That is more evident in the Latin word for mercy, *Misericordia,* "sad at heart." But there is one very important point to be cleared up before we consider the necessity of giving alms. True charity includes not only the obligation of mercy but also of justice to our neighbor. You do not love your neighbor if you do not treat him with justice. The Catechism of the Council of Trent, indeed, connects almsgiving with the Commandment "Thou shalt not steal," and declares that this commandment also implies the obligation to sympathize with the poor and needy.

This obligation of doing justice has never been put more strongly than in the labor Encyclical *Rerum Novarum* by Leo XIII, the Encyclicals *Quadragesimo Anno* and *Atheistic Communism* by Pius XI. Indeed, the whole theme of these masterly documents is justice and mercy. Thus Leo, while maintaining, contrary to the communistic idea, that "our first and most fundamental principle, therefore, when we undertake to alleviate the condition of the masses, must be the inviolability of private property," declares that the employer's "great and principal obligation is to give to everyone that which is just." And Pius XI, in the *Quadragesimo Anno,* speaking of the sad conditions before Leo's Encyclical, which he calls the "Magna Charta on which all Christian activities in social matters are ultimately based," says of the condition when wealth was arrayed against poverty: "This state of things was quite satisfactory to the wealthy, who looked upon it as the consequence of inevitable and natural economic laws, and who, therefore, were content to abandon to charity alone the full care of relieving the unfortunate, as though it were the task of charity to make amends for the violation of justice." Hence he demands, that "Every effort must therefore be made that fathers of families receive a wage sufficient to meet adequately ordinary domestic needs"; and wishes it to be made possible for wage earners, even "to attain to the possession of a certain modest fortune."

Pius XI is even stronger in his Encyclical on *Atheistic Communism,* which he calls "a pseudo-ideal of justice." "But charity," he says, "will never be true charity unless it takes justice into constant account. The Apostle teaches that 'he that loveth his neighbor hath fulfilled the Law,' and gives the reason: 'For, *thou shalt not commit adultery, thou shalt not kill, thou shalt not steal* — and if there be any other commandment, it is comprised in this word: Thou shalt *love thy neighbor as thyself*' (Rom. 13:8, 9). According to the Apostle, then, all the commandments including those which are of strict justice, as those which forbid us to kill or steal, may be reduced to the single precept of true charity. From this it follows that a 'charity' which deprives the workingman of the salary to which he has a strict title in justice, is not charity at all, but only its empty name and hollow semblance. The wage-earner is not to receive as alms what is his due in justice. And let no one attempt with trifling charitable donations to exempt himself from the great duties imposed by justice. Both justice and charity often dictate obligations touching on the same subject-matter, but under different aspects; and the very dignity of the workingman makes him justly and acutely sensitive to the duties of others in his regard."

True love of neighbor, then, demands that he be given justice, not a mere sop of alms. But in vain will you look for complete justice on this earth.

Further, Pope Leo XIII explains: "Let it be laid down in the first place that humanity must remain as it is. It is impossible to reduce human society to a level." The Socialists may do their utmost, but are striving against nature in vain. There naturally exist among men innumerable differences of the most important kind; people differ in capability, in diligence, in health, and in strength; and unequal fortune is a necessary result of inequality in condition. There will always be labor, he says: "In like manner, the other pains and hardships of life will have no end or cessation on this earth; for the consequences of sin are bitter and hard to bear, and they must be with man as long as life lasts. To suffer and endure, therefore, is the lot of humanity; let men try as they may, no strength and no artifice will ever succeed in banishing from human life the ills and troubles which beset it."

Pius XI furthers this thought in *Quadragesimo Anno:* "Now in effecting this reform, charity 'which is the bond of perfection' (Col. 3:14) must play a leading part. How completely deceived are those inconsiderate reformers, who, zealous only for commutative justice, proudly disdain the help of charity. Charity cannot take the place of justice unfairly withheld, but even though a state of things be pictured in which every man receives at last all that is his due, a wide field will nevertheless remain open for charity. For justice alone, even though most faithfully observed, can remove, indeed, the cause of social strife, but can never bring about a union of hearts and minds."

The Popes, therefore, while insisting upon justice, know that there will always be the poor and unfortunate, and always the need of the better off coming to their assistance. It is an attitude as old as Christianity, and going even beyond that, to the beginning of God's dealings with mankind. The duty of almsgiving and of other works of mercy is reiterated in the Sacred Scripture.

One can choose, almost at random from the three hundred texts. Not to load the page with numberless quotations, we may take the following as typical of what is repeated over and over: "He that hath mercy on the poor lendeth to the Lord; and he will repay him" (Prov. 19:17). "If thy enemy be hungry, give him to eat: if he thirst, give him water to drink. For thou shalt heap hot coals upon his head, and the Lord will reward thee" (Prov. 25:21–22).

There is this striking passage from Tobias (4:7–12), which may be said to contain the whole theology of almsgiving: "Give alms out of thy substance, and turn not away thy face from any poor person: for it shall come to pass that the face of the Lord shall not be turned from thee. According to thy ability be merciful. If thou have much, give abundantly; if thou have little, take care even so to bestow willingly a little. For thus thou storest up to thyself a good reward for the day of necessity. For alms deliver from all sin, and from death, and will not suffer the same to go into darkness. Alms shall be a great confidence before the Most High God to all them that give it."

It was high teaching, as every word of God must be whether in the Old or New Testament. And, as we have seen, there was among the Jews in our Lord's time a great deal of generous giving. The Talmud says, "The rich help the poor in this world, and the poor help the rich in the other world." We are told that the Hebrew language has no less than fifteen different expressions for the one idea of gift, and that every contract, personal or national, had to be prefaced by a gift. We have already noted that the Hebrew word for alms meant holiness, or righteousness. And it was a practical assistance, not merely a theoretical one. Although there was little organized charity, as the term is popularly used today, there developed after the Captivity a special system for the collecting of alms every day in the synagogues.

Simon, the Just, a celebrated Jewish Doctor of the second century, B.C., said: "The world rests on three things, The Law, worship, and works of mercy." There was, indeed, almsgiving enough, and the Jews always practiced charity among themselves, but, be it remembered, to no one else. Generally speaking, at the time of our Lord almsgiving had degenerated into a mere mechanical and external gesture, a social rather than a religious action. The heart had gone out of it. It had no real piety behind it, no giving for the love of God or real love for neighbor, and hence it had little or no moral value. As for real pity, it was dead, especially among the Rabbis, who were the teachers of the people. And, like priests, like people. For instance, the Rabbis forbade the leper to wash his face — even stoned him as a menace. One Rabbi, and he is typical, would not eat an egg bought in a street where there was leprosy. More, they forbade the wiping of a wound on the Sabbath. Our Lord knew the low estate into which charity had fallen. He excoriated the leaders, who had betrayed the high teachings of the Scriptures. Beware of the Scribes, He cried, "who devour the houses of the widows, making pretence of long prayers" (Mark 12:40); though one of the Scribes had answered Him that "to love one's neighbor as oneself is a greater thing than all holocausts and sacrifices" (Mark 12:33).

But Christ did not merely condemn the lack of charity. He was Love itself. "O Thou Treasurer of the poor," cried St. Teresa. He was not the God of Plato who cynically declared, "God has no commerce with man." He was Love and Mercy, hence no need appealed to Him in vain. He healed countless ills, the lame, the blind, the deaf, the dumb, the palsied; He even raised the dead to life. And He gave those same powers to His apostles and disciples. He brought the poor and unfortunate back to their rightful place in the Kingdom of God. His was a Gospel of Mercy and Kindness. Even John the Baptist announced it — "Let him who has two tunics share with him who has none; and let him who has food do likewise" (Luke 3:11). Jesus took to Himself the Messianic prophecy of Isaias: "to bring good news to the poor he has sent me, to proclaim to the captives release, and sight to the blind. To set at liberty the oppressed" (Luke 4:19). So He declared His Beatitude of Mercy: "Blessed are the merciful, for they shall obtain mercy" (Matt. 5:7).

"He who receives you, receives me; and he who receives me receives him who sent me. He who receives a prophet because he is a prophet, shall receive a prophet's reward; and he who receives a just man because he is a just man, shall receive a just man's reward. And whoever gives to one of these little ones but a cup of cold water to drink because he is a disciple, Amen, I say to you, he shall not lose his reward" (Matt. 10:42). St. Mark has it: "For whoever gives you a cup of water to drink in my name because you are Christ's, amen, I say to you, he shall not lose his reward" (9:40).

Again: "Sell what you have and give alms. Make for yourselves purses that do not grow old, a treasure unfailing in heaven" (Luke 12:33). "But when thou givest a feast, invite the poor, the crippled, the lame, the blind: and blessed shalt thou be, because they have nothing to repay thee with; for thou shalt be repaid at the resurrection of the just" (Luke 14:13). Christ had no idea of establishing a material millennium where there would be no poverty, no pain. The Cross was His standard. "Blessed are the poor in spirit, for theirs is the Kingdom of Heaven." So He declared. "For the poor you have always with you, and whenever you want you can do good to them" (Mark 14:8).

But His strongest declaration about the necessity of giving alms and performing acts of mercy is in His description of the Last Judgment. "Then shall the King say to them that shall be on his right hand: Come, ye blessed of my Father, possess you the Kingdom, prepared for you from the foundation of the world. For I was hungry, and you gave me to eat; I was thirsty, and you gave me to drink; I was a stranger, and you took me in: Naked, and you covered me: sick, and you visited me: I was in prison and you came to me. Then shall the just answer him, saying: Lord, when did we see thee hungry, and fed thee; thirsty, and gave thee drink? And when did we see thee a stranger, and took thee in? Or naked, and covered thee? Or when did we see thee sick or in prison, and came to thee? And the King answering, shall say to them: Amen I say to you, as long as you did it to one of these my least brethren, you did it to me" (Matt. 25:34–40). And the damned are sent to Hell because they failed in these duties to Him: "Amen I say to you, as long as you did it not to one of these least, neither did you do it to me. And these shall go into everlasting punishment: but the just into life everlasting" (45–46).

Those astounding words contain the Charter of the Poor, the Charter of Almsgiving, from which are deduced the works of mercy.

The Apostles and, indeed, the Christian Church from its beginning until now, never fell away from that Charter. The *Acts of the Apostles* are filled with the relations of ministrations to the sick, of miracles of healing. Moreover there is a perpetual care of the needy. The early believers held all things in common, though this practice never was adopted outside of Jerusalem. It should be noted that there never was any communism about it, for Christianity ever considered private property inviolable. The system is related in *Acts* (4:34–36) "For neither was there any needy among them. For as many were owners of lands or houses, sold them, and brought the price of the things they sold, and laid it down before the feet of the Apostles. And distribution was made to everyone, according as he had need."

As for the giving of alms in the early Church, we read elsewhere: "And the disciples, every man according to his ability, purposed to send relief to the brethren who dwelt in Judea, which also they did, sending it to the ancients by the hands of Barnabas and Saul" (Acts 11:29–30). This was at the time of the famine in the reign of Emperor Claudius. St. Paul declared, "Now after several years I came to bring alms to my nation" (Acts 24:17). And again: "You yourselves know that these hands of mine have provided for my needs and those of my companions. In all things I have shown you that by so toiling you ought to help the weak and remember the word of the Lord Jesus, that he

himself said, 'It is more blessed to give than to receive' "
(Acts 20:35).

It was a generous charity, but not a slipshod one. It was
well organized, as is evident from the apopintment of
Deacons and Deaconesses. The Greek converts had protested to the Hebrews that their widows were neglected.
So, to remedy the neglect, Deacons were appointed, being
elected by the Christian Community at Jerusalem, to look
after the poor and the holding of the *Agape,* the common
meal where rich and poor ate together, share and share
alike, thus preserving the sense of Christian equality. The
Apostles had said: "It is not reason that we should leave
the word of God, and serve tables." Wherefore seven men
of good reputation were chosen, Stephen, Philip, Pro-
chorus, Nicanor, Simon, Parmenas and Nicolas. The word
"Deacon" merely meant minister, or servant, though later
it acquired a more definite meaning. As time went on the
duty of the Deacon, according to the Pontifical, was "to
minister at the altar, to baptize, and to preach." In addi-
tion to his duties at the Mass, he was a kind of overseer,
to let the Bishop know the state of his flock, to collect the
offertory at Mass, to visit the confessors who were imprisoned for the faith, to write the accounts of the Acts
of the Martyrs, etc. In similar work among the women —
although, of course, they were never in sacred orders —
certain widows and Deaconesses were appointed. The
Deaconesses assisted in the baptism of women, gave them
instruction, and visited those who were sick or in prison.

The office of Deaconess was abolished in the Western
Church in the tenth century, but it is still preserved in
the Syrian Church. The Bishop was the head of all this
charitable work. St. Paul, writing to Titus, says a Bishop
must be "hospitable, gentle, reserved, just, holy, conti-
nent" (Titus 1:9). Notice, he puts "hospitable" first. The
care of the poor and the sick, then, shows a solid, if limited, organization in the early Church. Collections were

taken up weekly for the clergy, the poor, and for the material upbuilding of the Church — much as they are today. We learn from St. Paul that general collections were taken up. He writes (1 Cor. 16:1–3), "Now concerning the collections that are made for the saints, as I have given order to the churches of Galatia, so do ye also. On the first day of the week let everyone of you put apart with himself laying up what it shall well please him: that when I come, the collections be not then to be made. And when I shall be with you, whomsoever you shall approve by letters, them will I send to carry your grace (gift) to Jerusalem." For the purpose of making collections, there were alms boxes in the church, as our poor boxes at the present day, while there was also a special chest, or *corban,* for collections on special days.

The Apostles, then, had learned well from the Lord the need of being kind to the poor, for from the very beginning they established the relief system. They preached almsgiving incessantly. The texts about it in the Epistles are too numerous to quote. St. Paul could say to the Corinthians (2 Cor. 11:8) "I stripped other churches, taking pay from them so as to minister to you." He was forever concerned about collections for the poor, talking them up, urging the entertainment of strangers, practising compassion for the imprisoned, standing up for the poor slaves, exercising fraternal correction. He was, indeed, the great Apostle of Charity, and every one of the works of mercy, corporal and spiritual, can be traced in his admonitions. St. John Chrysostom noted this. He said — "Let us make St. Paul mount into this holy pulpit with us, that great procurator of all the poor; there is not one of his Epistles where he does not recommend the poor. He knew how important was this duty."

It was the same with St. Peter who writes, "But above all things have a constant mutual charity among yourselves; for charity covers a multitude of sins. Be hospitable to one another without murmuring" (1 Pet. 4:7–10). Then there is the famous text from St. James (1:27) "Religion pure and undefiled before God the Father is this: to give aid to orphans and widows in their tribulation and to keep oneself unspotted from this world."

The teaching of Christ, the teaching of the Apostles, in regard to the practical relief of the poor, has never failed in the Church. Indeed, the Gospel spread so rapidly because it was the Gospel to the poor. It was the Gospel of Christ; it is the Gospel of the Church. Said Pius XI, in the Encyclical on *Atheistic Communism:* "Go to the working man, especially where he is poor, and in general go to the poor." The Jewish world, as we have seen, had need of that Gospel, but the pagan world especially needed it. Paganism, except in isolated cases, took little care of the poor. Man, of course, in all elements and all times has a certain quality of natural pity. But the multitude of pagans had little mercy, and in the cases where civic help was given, it was solely from a political or economic motive, surely not from a spiritual one. There must be true religion in order to have true charity. Thus the Pelagian heretics, nominally Christian, called mercy a vice, while the Manicheans considered kindness to the poor the work of an enemy. St. Augustine said of the Manicheans, "While they believe that bread weeps, they will not give it to a man whom they see weeping," and, "though they behold a man dying from hunger, they will forbid their disciples to give him bread, and will have more compassion on a cucumber than a man." If this was so even with those who still had left some traces of Christianity, conditions in pagan society were far worse. In early Greece and Rome, for instance, there was little regard for children, and deformed children were destroyed. Even Aristotle said: "When there were too many — for in our state population has a limit — the babe or unborn child was destroyed."

This was not always the case, however. As the sense of
the importance of the family grew away from the tribal
idea, there was the dawning of a sense of responsibility
for the child. Thus Plato advised that orphans be placed
under public guardians: "Men should have a fear of the
loneliness of orphans, and of the souls of the departed,
who by nature take a special care of their own children.
A man should love the unfortunate orphan of whom he is
guardian as if he were his own child; he should be as
careful and diligent in the management of the orphan's
property as of his own — or even more careful still." But
this occasional concern for the orphan, the poor, the sick
— and there were even public granaries and other helps
for relief, even quasihospitals in the temples of Greece
and Rome — was motivated solely by political, civic ends.
The aim of such help was to preserve the citizenhood.
Even the private liberality and the mutual-help societies
were all animated by civic ideals, to help the state, to increase its efficiency, to increase the man power. Heads
were counted, not souls. There was no Divine motive, no
conception of man as a fellow child of God. Hence, when
the Church with its new doctrine of the dignity of man,
and the blessedness of the poor, came into such a society,
a society at least half slave, it found that the most promis-
ing harvest was among the poor, even among the slaves.
The Church went to the poor, and suddenly the Kingdom
of God was established. The God of Mercy had given His
greatest alms to the world.

Chapter III

The Church and Alms

THE apostolic system of caring for the poor laid the foundations of our present system in the Church. All the varied and multiple activities, orphanages, asylums, hospitals, St. Vincent de Paul Conferences, and so on, are but necessary variations of the fundamental theme: "Go to the Poor!"

But at no time in the history of the Church was the duty of giving alms more insisted upon than in the first ages, when the memory of Christ and His apostles was as of yesterday. Even the pagans knew Christ's reputation for charity. Lucian, in his "Death of Peregrinus," speaking of Jesus as the "Crucified Sophist," says that He was the great lawgiver of the Christians and that He had ordered them to regard themselves as brothers and to practise the most perfect charity toward one another.

With the Christian there was the conviction that if he had riches from God it was his duty to distribute them for God. The Christian was but God's treasurer. He did not consider it an extraordinary task. His life was necessarily simple, his wants were few, he scorned luxury and unnecessary comforts. Luxury was pagan. We find the Fathers, such as Clement and Cyprian, condemning the too luxurious lives of the pagans.

In post-Apostolic days, with which we are now dealing, the Christian knew that when his simple wants were provided for, it was his duty to give of his superfluity, great or little, to the poor. So at Mass on Sunday and certain feast days he placed on the altar at the time of the Epistle his gift of money or food, as a gift to God. There were also chests in the Church for his offering. It should be noted that no offering was accepted from a bad Christian. The gifts, at Mass or in the chests, as well as the proceeds from the property which some Christians voluntarily sold, and the dues collected, which after the time of Constantine developed into the tithe system, were given to the Bishop for distribution through the deacons, subdeacons, and deaconesses. By this method of secret distribution the self-respect of the poor was protected. There was no room for chance begging or idleness, for only the deserving poor were helped. In return the recipients were expected to pray for the donors. The whole process was a necessary one considering the times, especially once the continual persecutions began. The Christians then were a race apart; they were pariahs, suspected of being enemies of the state, and hence they were calumniated and persecuted, and faced martyrdom every day. Many of them believed that the end of the world was near, and for that reason they minimized the daily life of sacrifice and pain, spending their time in prayer and fasting. In such conditions, what sense would there be in piling up worldly wealth? They did not want it anyway. Poverty was blessed. It was a day to day existence, therefore it was easy enough. To share with one another was just a part of daily life. And this brotherly aid, which included all the works of mercy, was extended to their Christian brethren who lived afar, and even to pagans. Christian charity was not a closed corporation.

The practice of the early Christians in giving alms is evidenced on every page of the writings of the Fathers. The Fathers did not mince words. There is even a danger in taking their words too literally. Some Communists have done that and have asserted that St. Augustine, St.

Ambrose, and others were opposed to private property. That charge is untrue, unjust. The Fathers insisted on the right of private property in terms as strong as those of Leo XIII and Pius XI, while their words on alms-giving at times call for careful interpretation. Often their own statements in other passages contribute the proper explanation. Says St. Ambrose: "If you give to a poor man, you do not share with him what belongs to you, but you return to him what is his. For you have usurped what was given for the common use of all." And St. Gregory the Great declared: "When we minister some necessary things to the needy we do not give them what is ours, but we give them back what is theirs, thus complying with an obligation of justice rather than performing a work of mercy." So St. Augustine: "It is no greater crime to take from one who has, than when you are able and abound to refuse the needy. — If you have not fed, you have killed. Those are not a man's goods which he cannot take with him; mercy alone is the companion of the dead."

How many such passages, as already hinted, which seem to imply that the wealthy are guilty of robbery if they do not give alms, may be considered in some cases as rhetorical, in order to stir up the rich to their duty; or they may be justly interpreted as applying to such cases as Pius XI, for example, speaks of, where almsgiving will not take the place of justice.

Christ, while condemning the mammon of iniquity, that is the riches of iniquity, did not condemn wealth in itself. He even declared that it may be used to lay up treasures in Heaven, and that while too often it can be the occasion of moral destruction, it can acquire also, when used aright, many spiritual blessings. Thus St. Augustine, while he followed the rule of Evangelical poverty, did not insist on everyone else doing so, however desirable it was. "Let the rich," he says, "use what their infirmity has accustomed them to; but let them be sorry that they are not able to do otherwise. For it would be better for them if they could." He said scornfully to the pagan Romans, "You are depraved by prosperity, and you cannot be reformed by adversity." But he declares plainly that St. Paul "reprehends the desire after riches only, not the use of them." So though he preached indifference to riches, he warned those who practised voluntary poverty not to condemn the rich Christians by whose very charity they were sustained. Leo XIII seems to have had that in mind when he wrote, "Money and the other things which men call good and desirable — we may have them in abundance or we may want them altogether; as far as eternal happiness is concerned, it is no matter; the only thing that is important is to use them aright."

"Money is vile," says St. Ambrose, "but mercy is precious." If there were no wealth there could be no alms.

There was need of such teaching in Augustine's time, for Rome then consisted of a few patrician families ministered to by a multitude of slaves. So the thing he insisted upon was to share the wealth by charity, in a Christian, not a communistic way. And so insisted St. John Chrysostom in almost identical words. There has always been the question which is more provocative of evil, excess of wealth or excess of poverty. It is hard to decide. The evil in both is the excess. St. Francis of Assisi said, "Money is unto the servants of God nought else than the devil and a poisonous serpent"; and "Poverty is an especial way to salvation." But he was speaking to those who had wed Lady Poverty. Our Lord said to St. Catherine about those who were too much attached to worldly things, "Had they held them as things lent to them and not as their own, they would leave them without pain." Just there is the true idea of wealth — "things lent." St. John is said to have declared that the contempt of riches is meritorious only when the rejected riches benefit the poor.

Not only did the Fathers insist upon the obligation of giving alms, but they were forever preaching its beneficent influence upon the soul of the dispenser of mercy. "Mercy," says St. Augustine, "is the compassion in our heart of another's misery, by which, if we can, we are compelled to alleviate it." Compelled! But, "the quality of mercy is not strain'd." He goes on: "The prayers of the poor are my defence; those blind, those lame, those aged persons, are more powerful than the stoutest warriors."

The Fathers went so far as to call almsgiving "another baptism." St. Jerome says: "Such alms cleanse the soul as by an immersion; the fire of hell is extinguished by the sacred font, and the worm of conscience is destroyed by the pious liberality which relieveth Christ in the poor." And St. John Chrysostom asserts, "If virginity should want the works of mercy, it will be cast out with the impure."

And so, building on the Gospels, Epistles, and writings of the Fathers, the solid theology of almsgiving was established. The obligation of giving alms was always recognized as a simple Christian duty, but its particular application was learned the hard way, by experience. Alms must be in proportion to current wretchedness. Just as soon as the Church was freed by Constantine and came up out of the Catacombs, the demands upon her became greater since she had to help not only her own children but the pagans as well. Well did she do that work. Julian the Apostate said, "It is a shame that the Galileans nourish their poor and ours." It is like to what Luther said to the people of Wittenberg: "God has given you the Word in all its purity; notwithstanding, I see no charity in you."

In those early ages of Christianity civic officers were in a bad condition. Everywhere there was corruption in government, extravagance, usury, disdain of the poor, even cruelty to them; and then with the invasion of the Barbarians there was more want than had ever been experienced before. Either the original system of gathering alms, which had prevailed during the persecutions, was not effective enough — the faith was colder — or on account of the depression there was not as much money to give. Too much taxation always hurt charitable enterprises. Consequently, with the increased need, we find more urging to give alms, and when people did not willingly respond there was eventually — as in the seventh century — the necessary resort to tithes, practically another tax. But, making up for the alms of the ordinary people, there were more princely donations from the very wealthy and from the Emperors.

The revenues of the Church, from whatever source, were the main treasury of alms for the poor. These church revenues were beautifully called the "Patrimony of the Poor." They were divided into four parts: for the Bishop and his needs; for the support of the clergy; for the upkeep of worship, or propagation of the faith; and for those in need — the sick, the aged, the orphans, the poor, the hospitals, asylums, orphanages, and other charitable institutions. Hence one fourth of the revenue was for the needy. Relief had to be found for them anyway, even if the sacred vessels had to be sold. St. Ambrose, St. Augustine — it is common in the lives of the saints — sold the sacred vessels to feed the poor. This division of revenue was the general custom in Rome in the fifth century, and soon became universal. In fact almost every work of mercy in the world today is of Christian origin and goes back to those early days when the poor were the Church's treasure. When the persecutors demanded of St. Lawrence — who was a Deacon — the treasures of the Church, he pointed to the poor whom he had fed and clothed, and said, "These are the treasures, in whom is Christ, in whom is faith."

From all this system of almsgiving and from the Church's perpetual preaching of the obligation, we can readily advance to the theology of the works of mercy.

The first thought to grasp is that poverty in itself is neither good nor bad. It may be, and often is, a terrible evil, destructive of all spirituality; and that is why the Popes have fought against involuntary indigence. Poverty, too, may be a blessing, when voluntary. "Blessed are the poor in spirit," does not necessarily imply a state of *actual* poverty. Yet Christ belonged to a poor family, though the poverty of the Holy Family was not indigence or destitution. St. Joseph was a good provider. St. Bernard ingeniously thinks that our Lady gave to the poor the gold received from the Magi, or perhaps saved it for the sojourn in Egypt. It may be noted, too, that the women who aided Christ and the Apostles were wealthy women. But Christ chose to be poor, and urged upon the rich youth whom He loved to sell what he had, give to the poor, and follow Him. He should thus have treasures in heaven. He loved the poor and blessed them. That is why St. Francis called poverty "Christ's widow." The poor have been called the first-born of the Church.

St. John Chrysostom draws a parallel of two cities, the city of the rich, and the city of the poor. The poor city, he says, will be stronger, because it will be more laborious and more virtuous. There is no such political city, of course, but this City of the Poor is found in the Church. Christ gives them the first place there. "Bring in hither the poor, and the feeble, and the blind and the lame" (Luke 14:21). "He hath anointed me to preach the Gospel to the poor" (Luke 4:18). And St. James says: "Hath not God chosen the poor in this world, rich in faith and heirs of the Kingdom" (3:5).

Just as poverty in itself is neither good nor bad, so, too, is it with wealth, as we have already seen. But there is a great danger in riches. Our Lord made it very clear that it is especially hard for a rich man to save his soul. No matter how you look at riches, even when you "use them aright," riches are a burden. It is the tyranny of things. As St. Augustine says: "Not to have the burden of poverty is to have the greater one of riches." But if riches — and we speak of comparative riches, not the wealth of the multimillionaire — are to be an asset to a man, instead of being a liability, they must be used properly, as a trust. They come from God, they must in some way go back to God. "It is one thing to have a right to possess money," says Leo XIII, "and another to have a right to use money as one pleases." The only way to use it is for God. The definition of alms is: "A work by which something is given to a needy one, *on account of God*."

So alms is given for God's sake, a fact which distinguishes Christian alms from mere pagan philanthropy. The meaning of true charity is love of neighbor for God's sake; real love, not merely not to do or wish evil to him, but to have at heart his interests, to be really one with him, our love for him being after the model of our love for ourselves. It is easy enough to wish well to a man, but not so easy to make a sacrifice for him.

It is of prime importance for us to know from what we shall draw our alms for our neighbor. It may be broadly stated that we are obliged to give out of our superfluity to others who are in need. St. Thomas says: "I say superfluous not only in respect to one's self, which is above that which is necessary to the individual, but also in respect to others the care of whom falls upon him; in respect of whom it is necessary to the person inasmuch as it is necessary to the dignity of that person; because it is first necessary that one should provide for himself, and those of whom he has the care, and afterwards, from the residue, help the needs of others."

To put it plainly, first of all a man can provide for himself and dependents, to live according to their station

in life. Out of what is left — the superfluous — he is obliged
to aid a person who is in extreme need, and also aid the
community in grave need. He is not obliged to give all
his superfluous wealth but only a part of it. There is, of
course, the danger of minimizing the superfluous and
exaggerating what we feel is necessary to our state of life.
St. Augustine says, "We have much superfluous if we
only keep the necessaries, for if we seek luxuries, nothing
suffices." St. Basil excoriated the rich of his day — "Cruel,
they take away necessities from the poor, to give dainty
and superfluous things to their own belly."

This matter of superfluity needs to be modified. If a
neighbor is in extreme want, for example, in danger of
perishing, or in the case where common good demands,
even the poor man is obliged to help, though he himself
suffer actual privation in doing so. Needless to say, no
one is bound to give to others what is required for his
own immediate necessities. But he who refuses to give
according to his means when appealed to by one in extreme need, and who at the same time is the only one who
can give, can be guilty of a mortal sin.

As to the amount of his superfluous wealth that a man
is obliged to give, it is pretty hard to say. Some say that
two per cent is enough, while others demand more. There
is no rigid rule. It depends upon the need to be treated,
so that the greater the need, the more one is bound to
give. Need may be extreme, as in danger of life; quasi-
extreme, as in danger of mutilation, etc.; grave, as danger
of captivity, or danger of great loss of goods; and finally,
light need, which is ordinary poverty. A great liberality,
thus, is required only in cases of extreme necessity. In
other cases a moderate generosity is sufficient. Father
Faber, however, asks the question, "With what amount
of generosity?" And he replies, "One word answers that
question — God." And he goes on: "I conclude with one
more grave truth. I said fewer rich were saved than poor:

I now add that the great multitudes of the rich who are lost are lost principally because they are stingy, irregular, or fanciful. I beg of you to mark the three words — stingy, irregular, or fanciful, in their mercy to the poor."

Sometimes, it is true, the rich leave some of their wealth to the poor. Some of these would take it with them, if they could. An old spiritual writer said: "Note well that it is better for you to give during your life one penny for the honor of God than a mountain of gold after your death. On a dark road you do not place the lantern behind your back." There is a story told of St. Lucy. She wanted her mother to give her dowry to the poor, but the mother told her to wait and give her money when she died. Lucy replied: "That which you give at death you give because you cannot take it with you. But if you give it in your lifetime you will have the reward in the world to come." So they gave all to the poor. Lucy's betrothed was so enraged that he denounced her to the pagan authorities, and she was put to death. There was a slogan popular a few years ago: "Do it now!" Surely it is a good motto for the giving of alms.

Without too much refining on required percentages, the one aim for every Christian, rich and poor, is to give as generously as possible. Someone has said, "Do not allow the mind to stifle the sentiments of the heart." It is a good corrective of the tendency to minimize in doing charity. It is to give gladly, willingly, with a spiritual intention; it is to give from the pure motive of love of God and neighbor, not out of a purely natural sympathy. William, Count of Poitou, once gave a church. He said, "I make this gift because I remember my sins, because I would that God might forget them." As St. John Chrysostom put it: "Alms have wings, they confer the lightness and elasticity of angels." According to St. Francis the bread of beggars was blessed and sanctified by charity. St. Anthony of Padua said: "Alms in Holy Scripture are termed a sack because whatever you put in it is found in the eternal life. Thou art a stranger, O man! Carry this sack on the way of thy pilgrimage, that in the evening when thou arrivest at the hospice, thou mayest have some provision."

To give alms properly is to give them without ostentation, not letting the left hand know what the right hand does; it is to give with discretion, not in a haphazard way, but with due regard for the present need of the poor. The old saw is still good religion: "He gives twice who gives quickly." Generally speaking, indiscriminate giving that encourages beggary is not true charity. There is even the danger of spoiling with kindness. St. Francis never spared the loafer who lived at ease on the goodness of others. He insisted on labor and service. Only in rare cases would he permit his friars to accept money. He well might have coined the old proverb, "Never set an empty pot on the fire hoping your neighbor will come to fill it."

But even while discretion may be necessary, it can be overdone. It may be a cloak for stinginess. Charity is often abused; what of it? "Endeavor to be charitable only by your reason," says an old ascetic writer, "and you will endeavor in vain." The poor have rights not only to our money, but to our kindness. That is the least you can give. "If you can give," says St. Augustine, "give; if you cannot, be affable; God crowns a good will where He does not find the work." We are told that St. Andrew Corsini was very kind to the poor, "especially the bashful among them." What a lovely charity that was! There is no excuse for refusing to give alms from the fear that you may be fooled. There are plenty of charities absolutely safe. There is the local St. Vincent de Paul Society. There are the many diocesan institutions for the alleviation of every distress, there is the Society for the Propagation of the Faith. There are needs enough if you have the generosity. You do not need to go out looking for someone to aid. If you had to do that, you would rarely find occasion for your alms. But the occasion is at your door all the time in our wonderful Catholic charities. The constant marvel is that they function so well. They have few endowments from the rich. Like the local parish, they depend almost entirely on the generosity of the ordinary Catholic. The Church is the Church of the poor in more ways than one.

And if we live, if we are blessed with the Faith, if we enjoy so many material and spiritual blessings, it is because Holy Mother Church, like the Mother of God, has been to us ever the Mother of Mercy.

Chapter IV

The Works of Mercy

THE Church, as Mother of Mercy, has made almsgiving her own peculiar science. Always proclaiming its obligation, she has not dealt with it in a general, cursory manner, but has sounded the duty to the very bottom. She is not content with a general exhortation; she goes into details, lest, perhaps, she might unwittingly overlook some of her distressed children. She is the seeker rather than the sought. Thus she has charted the works of mercy, spiritual and corporal. All of them, as is evident, are founded on the life and teaching of Jesus Christ. They are practical guides to Christianity, to the imitation of Christ.

The corporal works of mercy, for instance, are practically all noted verbatim in His exhortation concerning the Last Judgment: "I was hungry and you gave me to eat, etc." This scientific enumeration of the details of Christian alms, therefore, is not modern. It is Scriptural, hence it was not overlooked by the Fathers. Even in their writings — particularly in those of Lactantius and St. Augustine — the corporal works are enumerated just as you find them in our little catechism today. St. Augustine, however, omits the specific mention of visiting the sick, although he very likely includes that under one of the other Scriptural commands. But it is during the Middle Ages — called by Digby "ages of mercy, ages of charity or love" — that we find the works of mercy systematized. In those days every word of Scripture was meditated upon and fitted into the theological system. St. Thomas gathered all that learning to himself and used his mighty intellect, his deep faith and love, to make all a living, practical science. Thus while others were familiar with the enumeration of the works of mercy, he, as it were, made them permanent, unchanging. He established them in their present form. He enumerates the corporal works: To feed the hungry, to give drink to the thirsty, to clothe the naked, to harbor the harborless, to visit the sick, to redeem the captive, to bury the dead. You will note a little difference in the order from that in which we recite them, but they are all there in identical words. It should be remembered that St. Thomas was chiefly a practical professor. He was considering his students, not making a reference book for future ages. He was too humble to aspire to that. So to make it easier for his students, he summarized the works in this Latin verse:

Vestio, Poto, Cibo, Redimo, Tego, Colligo, Condo.

The requirements of the verse made it necessary to change the order a bit.

He enumerates, also, the spiritual works of mercy: To teach the ignorant, to counsel the doubtful, to comfort the sorrowful, to correct the sinner, to forgive offenses, to bear heavy or grave wrongs, to pray for all. And again he makes a helpful Latin verse:

Consule, Castiga, Solare, Remitte, Doce, Fer, Ora.

It is hard to draw absolute lines of separation. The soul is more important than the body, and so the spiritual works of mercy are more eminent than the corporal; nevertheless, you can see where at times the corporal in a specific case would be more compelling. If a man is starving, for instance, he needs food and not fraternal correction. But, in general, the spiritual works are more important, since they concern the eternal rather than the temporal welfare of our neighbor. It is not enough to concentrate on our own salvation. We all have certain duties in regard to the salvation of others, duties either of charity or justice, though here again it should be said that we cannot save our own souls without doing our duties toward the salvation of others. Thus St. Vincent de Paul said that to help the body was only to accomplish half the task imposed by the virtue of charity, of love of God and man. To assist the soul in the journey through life on its passage to eternity is even more essential. And the great lay apostle, Frederick Ozanam, who practised all the works of mercy, time and again exhorted the members of the St. Vincent de Paul Society to consider the spiritual helps they could give even more than the material relief. The comfort of the body is only secondary. Not only is there the obligation for us to do the works of mercy, but it is a command with a promise. Do them and you will be blessed; omit them and you will be counted among the wicked.

The Christian purpose in doing them should be for the sake of Christ, in imitation of Him, and as a means to be united with Him forever. To imitate Him is to be safe; it is the purchase price of glory. It is a sure investment, unfailing as buying good bonds. There is a beautiful letter on this subject written by an Italian nobleman to the great Lorenzo de Medici: "God, my Lorenzo, is venal; but with what money can the great God be bought? Oh, with that with which He bought others, that is, charity, with charity to the poor, for before Him we are all poor, indeed; and He hath bought, He hath redeemed us. Let no one, wise, or brave, or temperate boast that he imitates God. These are but shadows of Divine virtue. Only the man bountiful to the poor exactly imitates Him. O happy merchant who with a small price buys both man and God!" It is a business transaction, big business, as our Lord puts it, and nothing should be allowed to interfere with it. In Paris, we are told, in the fourteenth century actors were forbidden to give plays during the special times set apart for collections for the poor, lest the money of the people be diverted from the poor. Business before pleasure, and the business of the poor came first. Rather was it God's business.

There was no danger of giving too much to the poor; no complex about the fear of being too easy, too merciful. Bernardine, a noted General of the Capuchins, said: "If God should call me to account in judgment for being too severe and inflexible, I should have nothing to answer for myself in defense; but if He should accuse me of being too clement and merciful, I should find an excuse instantly; for I could reply that I had learned mercy from Him, who had also exceeded measure in showing pity." It is like the saying of St. Gregory Nazianzen, "Be God to the suffering by imitating the mercy of God." It all boils down to this: Do mercy here to others, and you will get it for yourself hereafter. That is the whole command and promised reward. It is your citizenship paper for the Kingdom of God. As St. John Chrysostom said, "Gather your substance there where your country is."

There is scarcely a saint who does not view the giving of mercy in the light of a spiritual business proposition. It is not strange, since our Lord Himself put it in that wise. "Blessed are the merciful, for they shall obtain mercy." It is give and take all through. It is all put so prosily, simply, in order that we may have no alibi, no excuse.

St. Bonaventure, who held such a high place in the Franciscan adventure of the quest of poverty, was severe with himself but lenient with others. No work of mercy was foreign to him. His motive, too, was the very prosy one of spiritual self-seeking, a supernaturalized tit for tat. "By mercy," he said, "man merits in this world grace, in death confidence, in judgment mercy, in heaven glory." Centuries before, St. Jerome had given expression to a like thought: "I do not remember to have read of anyone dying a bad death who liberally exercised works of Charity; for such a one has many intercessors, and it is impossible that the prayers of these men are not heard." To do the works of mercy was to make a man Godlike. "Man has nothing so divine," says St. Gregory Nazianzen, "as to merit well of others." And St. Ambrose made mercy to others the essence of Christianity, "Nothing so commends a Christian as the mercy of Charity."

Oftentimes the saints had little to give. What, for example, can a nun in her cloister give? But they all had the will for the deed. They might not be able even to match the widow's mite, or the cup of cold water, but at least they could give many a prayer, and radiate mercy; and somehow if you concentrate on one work of mercy you may discover that you have been preaching them all, for the cloak of charity is seamless, all of one piece.

One thing that is repeated over and over in Scripture is that these works of mercy redeem from sin. Doing them to the poor, you do them to Christ, and consequently, to put it plainly, you put Him under a compliment to you. It seems almost blasphemous to say that, till you recall the very words of our Lord. St. John Chrysostom expresses that same idea: "The gift which you make to the poor establishes you as creditor of the Lord." The Lord is your debtor. He is under a compliment to you; express it as you will. Anyway we are debtors to the poor. Bossuet says: "The rich can save themselves only by the poor, because the poor are the first-born of the Church, because they hold the first places there, because they have its privileges." St. Augustine urges us to sell very dear what is of little value. Change money for the blessings of heaven — big business again. Some go so far as to say that the pursuit of the works of mercy is a sign of predestination. We can well believe it when we see the important place these works have in the science of the saints.

God, however, does not wait till eternity to reward the doer of mercy. The works of mercy effect their reward here in the giver as well as in the getter. But not necessarily in increase of material wealth. In the Old Testament God promised temporal blessings to His chosen people. He had to coax them along, so little removed were they from paganism. But it is not so in His Church. His followers are no longer children. They are supposed to have put away the things of a child. They are men, athletes, soldiers, training for heroism, even for martyrdom. And the sign He promised them was His own Cross. Yet when all is said there is a true heroism about doing the works of mercy. They are a conquest of self; some of them, like forgiving injuries, are a real martyrdom. Unselfishness is always heroic. But apart from the high spiritual victory, there is a true happiness, a self-satisfaction in doing any work of mercy, when you know that you are contributing to the well-being of the individual or of the community. In that sense virtue is its own reward. There is a glow about doing a work of mercy that makes you feel good all over. You lose nothing — for giving never yet made the giver any poorer — but you gain in stature even in your own estimation. It is not pride, but comfort. There is even a worldly honor shown to such a man, no matter how humble his own motives. "The rich man who gives alms," says St. John Chrysostom, "is honored, cherished as a father; he shares with God the titles by which gratitude expresses itself, the titles of Savior and Benefactor." One could not demand a higher title for doing a few acts of kindness.

A nation is blessed that trades in the works of mercy. Johnson said that the real criterion of civilization consists in the degree of provision made for the happiness of the poor. All in all, that is what made the Middle Ages so particularly Catholic — that their chief concern was the searching out of cases where the works of mercy would have sway. That is sound theology. St. Bernardine of Siena said: "If we investigate the reason and cause of mercy, we shall find that it includes in itself the perfection of all virtues."

Since that is so, the daily cultivation of the works of mercy is of supreme importance in the spiritual life. They must be cultivated daily. It will not do just to wait for the chance case of a beggar who needs a handout. It is poor charity that is satisfied with buying a pencil from a blind man. Mercy must be pursued in order to be caught and taken to ourselves. The more you do in that line, the more you will want to do. The old advice is, "Give so that you may get the grace to give more." It never fails. It is as if God were egging you on and trying to make you match His own generosity. But it is not as easy as it looks. It needs the Divine urge, the drive of the Holy Ghost.

To so many people the world of mercy is a foreign planet. They readily discover excuses to explain away their neglect of the works of mercy. Every man for himself, they say; I must think of the future; I must provide for my family; I never bother with my neighbors; I am a self-made man, and no one ever gave me a lift; and so on. It is always I — I — I. It is the magnifying of self, the valuation that leaves even God out of the equation. Yet that selfish spirit is tempting God. No selfish man, no self-sufficient man, can grasp the idea of the Providence of God. Let God take away His hand, and where are you? Worldly prosperity is at best an ephemeral thing. We have it today, we may lack it tomorrow. A visit to any institution for the care of the aged will make that a convincing lesson. There are many now in charitable institutions, through no fault of their own, who once had abundance. It was so in the time of St. John Chrysostom. "The poor also," he writes, "were formerly young, robust, rich perhaps; for who can ignore human vicissitudes. Far from insulting their misfortune, let us think, whoever we are, that it can happen to us, and let us not refuse them the tender assistance which is due to lowliness."

It is a good investment, then, to practise the works of mercy, a temporal investment as well as an eternal one. It is an investment in a fund that will never collapse, will never pass a dividend. God is too good a bookkeeper to fail to credit our account with what is due it. Or as St. Teresa puts it, "What a good Pay-master God is!" She was a fine example herself of an investor in the works of mercy. Her father had great charity to the poor and the sick. For instance, he never would keep slaves, although in his day it was considered quite proper to do so. Teresa, as a little girl, followed his example. "I gave alms as I could," she said, "and I could but little." Little, indeed, of material alms, but, as we shall see later, no saint was more lavish than she in doing the spiritual works of mercy. "I gave as I could." If she had had a million dollars, trust Teresa to have spent it all on the poor.

There is something about every saint that makes him impoverish himself for the welfare of his needy neighbor. So many saints — you might say, all the saints — gave all they had to the poor. When St. Cecelia was martyred the Roman Prefect demanded her wealth of Pope Urban. The Pope replied: "The wealth of Cecelia has long since flown to heaven by the hands of the poor." "All that I have," said St. Ambrose, "belongs to the poor." St. Gregory the Great wanted his people to regard the Church as the storehouse of the world. He provided for the poor everywhere, and was so generous that when he died his enemies sneered that there was nothing left in the treasury of the Church. Someone might have retorted that the real treasures of the Church were the treasures in heaven. And so that total concern with the works of mercy goes on through all the ages of the Church. St. Francis of Assisi and his friars gave to the poor everything they could lay their hands on. So many of the Franciscans, before wedding Lady Poverty, sold all their property and gave all the proceeds to the needy. It was so with St. Vincent de Paul. Once he was given money to buy a horse, but immediately he spent it all on the poor English and Irish Catholics who had fled to France from Cromwell. Someone should write a book on St. Vincent and the Irish. Give, give, give, was the motto of the saints. It was not merely to be relieved of the tyranny of things, but to give comfort to others. Therein was their joy. The famous director of souls, Abbé Huvelin, expressed it thus: "It is not what you give but what you retain that will cause you suffering." So, if we are to find the secret of the happiness of the saints, we must look to the works of mercy. The field is vast, the opportunities innumerable. The whole world is our parish. The one thing to remember is that truth which Pius XI declared in his Encyclical on *Atheistic Communism,* "that the peoples of the earth form but one family in God."

THE CORPORAL WORKS
OF MERCY

Chapter V

To Feed the Hungry

WHEN we think of poverty we think chiefly of the lack of food. The giving of alms to the poor man necessarily covers more than enough to eat. The great exemplars of charity, like St. John the Almoner, St. John of God, St. Francis of Assisi, St. Catherine of Siena, St. Vincent de Paul, were specialists in every work of mercy, corporal and spiritual alike. All the works are necessary, though insistence is put on food. Man is a social being. He has a right to a decent living, to all the comforts of food and clothing and lodging and to all the many other things that are necessary in order to live a civilized life.

As Pius XI, in his Encyclical on *Atheistic Communism,* puts it: "Man has been endowed by God with many varied prerogatives; the right to life, to bodily integrity, to the necessary means of existence; the right to tend toward his ultimate good in the path marked out for him by God; the right of association, and the right to possess and use property."

But while the giving of alms has the purpose of providing for all these things, there is a great value in specializing as to the various needs in order to make them more appealing to the mercy of his neighbor. It crystallizes the thought. Thus it is one thing to speak of helping a poor man, but that generic appeal has not the same power as to ask for a loaf of bread to save a man who is dying of starvation.

So, to feed the hungry is made the leading corporal work of mercy because all in all it is the most vital. You could live without shelter, without clothes, in certain climates, but nowhere on earth could you live without food. You could, of course, live longer without food than you could without water. But eventually, and soon, you would die if you had nothing to eat. To avert that horrible agony of starvation a man finally will eat anything, even the offal which a brute animal will ignore. The innumerable tales in our histories of the gruesome meals that the famine stricken partook of in order to try to hold on to life are testimonials to that fact. To read of the famines in Ireland in past years, of the famines which even now in China and India mow down millions, is a sickening experience, all the more horrible because such visitations seem so avoidable if we all exercised the spirit of charity. Famine in a world of plenty is an insult to the Providence of God. To win a war by starving innocent children is a costly victory when it destroys the very spirit of charity. You can pile up all the horrors at the siege of Jerusalem, but the one memory that will stand out is the history of the poor crazed mother who killed and ate her own infant. Today children are slaughtered for less obvious reasons. Herod is not the only tyrant whose hands are red with the blood of little ones.

So the thought of life brings the thought of food, as essential as the air we breathe. So in every language food, or bread, came to be the generic term for all bodily needs. The absolute need of it was connected with the primal curse after the fall of man. "In the sweat of thy face shalt thou eat bread till thou return to the earth, out of which thou wast taken" (Gen. 3:19). Our Lord deemed it sufficient to make just one reference to our temporal needs in the "Our Father," when He taught us to pray — "Give us this day our daily bread."

The duty of feeding the hungry is as old as man. Even natural mercy or sympathy would compel a man to that. You find it even among pagans, though they have only a natural religion or no religion at all. In the time of Homer, as you will find in the Iliad and the Odyssey, hospitality, both in Greece, and Rome, was the first public charity, and it was contrary to the law and the accepted religious beliefs to neglect the stranger. The host welcomed the visitor, gave him food and drink and shelter. In every great house there was a special table for strangers, who were not only entertained, but on their departure were presented with gifts, chiefly of food. And that hospitality was exercised also in the hovels of the poor. And if that was so among the pagans from a merely natural religion, it was far more obligatory to the believers in the true God.

All through the Old Testament this matter of feeding the hungry is taken as a matter of course. One of the most beautiful pictures is that of the two angels coming to visit Lot at Sodom (Gen. 19:1–3). Lot invited them into his house, to lodge there and wash their feet. And, "He made them a feast and baked unleavened bread, and they ate." The story of how Joseph averted the famine in Egypt is told at length in Genesis, but somehow that narrative is not as thrilling as the assurance he gave his brothers after the death of their father Jacob: "Fear not: I will feed you and your children" (Gen. 50:21).

The importance of food, and even the miraculous means which a Provident God will use to give it, is seen in the Exodus from Egypt when He sent down from heaven the daily Manna. "I will rain bread from Heaven for you" (Exod. 16:4). It is estimated by Biblical scholars that the amount of Manna was fifteen million pounds a week.

The Law of Moses provided for feeding the poor. This is seen especially in the command as to gleaning. "When thou reapest the corn of thy land, thou shalt not cut down all that is on the face of the earth to the very ground: nor shalt thou gather the ears that remain neither shalt thou gather the bunches of grapes that fall down in thy vineyard, but shalt leave them to the poor and the strangers alike" (Lev. 19:9–10). It was a gentle way of regarding the self-respect of the poor man. So strict was the law of feeding the hungry that the Lord declared that even the pagan Ammonite and the Moabite, even after the tenth generation, would not enter the church of the Lord forever: "Because they would not meet you with bread and water in the way when you came out of Egypt" (Deut. 23:3–4). And so it goes on. The Scriptures are a commentary on mercy. Boaz ordering his servants to let fall purposely handfuls of wheat so that Ruth might glean them without shame; Elias the prophet fed by the ravens; the Governor of the House of Achab hiding the hundred prophets in caves and feeding them there; Elias, again, when he was fleeing from the wrath of Jezebel fed with a hearth cake by an angel; Tobias, feeding the hungry, clothing the naked and burying the dead, as he declared the law of mercy: "Eat thy bread with the hungry and the needy" (4:17) — all these are beautiful idylls, charming literature, but they are vastly more: they are the history of God's Providence, the command of the Lord to men to imitate Him. One of the worst taunts that Eliphaz made to Job was the accusation — false, of course — that he had withdrawn bread from the hungry, and had sent widows away empty (Job 22:7–9).

It was not only a disgrace to neglect to feed the hungry. It was, too, a sin that cried to heaven for vengeance when there was question of defrauding laborers of their wages.

Over and over again the Psalmist sings of the mercy of God, "bringing forth grass for cattle and herb for the service of men," "wine to cheer the heart of man," "the fat of wheat," "the honey out of the rock," "the quail," "the bread of Heaven," "food to them that fear Him." God's goodness is even to the dumb animals. "All expect of thee that thou give them food in season" (103:27); "food to all flesh, for his mercy endureth forever" (135:25). The Book of Proverbs, in regard to the poor, reads like a text from the Sermon on the Mount: "If thy enemy be hungry give him to eat; if he thirst, give him water to drink. For thou shalt heap hot coals upon his head, and the Lord will reward thee" (25:21–22). How beautifully does the Book of Wisdom (16:20) speak of the Manna — "Thou didst feed thy people with the food of angels, and gavest them bread from heaven prepared without labor; having in it all that is delicious, and the sweetness of every taste"! It should be noted that these words are used for the versicles at Benediction of the Blessed Sacrament, the Bread from Heaven that fulfills the prophecy of the Manna.

So Ecclesiasticus warns: "Against him that is niggardly of his bread the city will murmur, and the testimony of his niggardliness is true" (31:29). And finally Isaias has this glorious tribute to the man who feeds the hungry: "Deal thy bread to the hungry, and bring the needy and the harborless into thy house: when thou shalt see one naked, cover him, and despise not thy own flesh . . . when thou shalt pour out thy soul to the hungry and shalt satisfy the afflicted soul, then shall thy light rise up in darkness, and thy darkness shall be as the noonday" (58:7, 10). The works of mercy are the chain of gold that runs through all the Scriptures from Genesis to Apocalypse.

But it is in the Gospels that we find the most beautiful lessons in regard to feeding the hungry. Herein is bread glorified, even transubstanced. The necessity of it as food is taken by our Lord to point many a spiritual lesson. Our Lady in her Magnificat sounded the mystery of God's Providence: "He has filled the hungry with good things." With our Lord, bread, as in the petition of the *Our Father,* stands not only as food for the life of the body but for the life of the soul. The whole thesis of His teaching is founded upon the figure of bread. It is this: God provides you with bread; you in turn must share it with your neighbor: if you do so, you will receive the Bread of Angels here and the Bread of Eternal Life hereafter. Bread comes from the soil; bread is changed into the flesh of man. There is a thought in some poet that in the course of ages all the earth will thus be transubstanced into man. It is a beautiful thought, but the reality is more beautiful still when the bread is transubstanced into the Body and Blood of Jesus Christ.

Our Lord's hearers could readily grasp — if they had the good will — his use of bread to convey a spiritual lesson. There was nothing commoner than bread. Barley bread was the food of the poor. This with fish was the ordinary diet. In Galilee especially our Lord was dealing with men who got their living by fishing. Bethsaida, a name we meet so often in the Gospels, meant fish house. Our Lord made use of the fisherman's skill to describe the search for souls. So the early writers called Him the "Divine Fisherman." We recall how commonly the picture of the fish, alone or with the baskets of bread, was used in the Catacombs as the type of Christ, the Greek letters being used acrostically for "Jesus Christ, Son of God, the Savior." But the Jews could understand better the references to bread than to fish. They recited this prayer before meals: "Blessed be Thou, Lord our God, who hast sanctified us by thy precepts and who bringest forth bread from the earth." They never forgot the Manna.

Our Lord, in one of His first teachings, made use of

the bread symbol. When at His temptation He was suffering from hunger after His fast of forty days, and the devil urged Him to turn the stones into bread, He replied, "Not by bread alone does man live; but by every word that comes forth from the mouth of God" (Matt. 4:3–4). He used it again in the Sermon on the Mount, to bring home the lessons of the Providence of God: "Look at the birds of the air: they do not sow or reap or gather into barns; yet your Heavenly Father feeds them. Are not you of much more value than they?" He taught them to pray for their "daily bread." Again He taught them about the fatherly love of God. "Or what man is there among you, who, if his son asks him for a loaf, will hand him a stone; or, if he asks for a fish, will hand him a serpent?" (Matt. 7:9–10.) There is finally the parable of the Great Supper: "But when thou makest a feast, call the poor, the maimed, the lame, and the blind; and thou shalt be blessed, because they have not wherewith to make the recompense; for recompense shall be made thee at the resurrection of the just" (Luke 14:13–14).

Not only did our Lord preach the need of bread, material and spiritual, not only did He order His followers to feed the hungry, but He Himself set the example of practical charity and fed them on a grand scale. One day He miraculously fed five thousand with five loaves and two fishes; on another day, four thousand with seven loaves and a few fishes. After the feeding of the five thousand, St. John (6) tells us that the people wanted to make Him King, but a material, not a spiritual King. Our Lord repulsed them and their materialism. "Amen, Amen, I say to you, you seek me, not because you have seen miracles, but because you did eat of the loaves, and were filled. Labor not for the meat which perisheth, but for that which endureth unto life everlasting, which the Son of Man will give you" (John 6:26–27). And then He went on to preach the glorious promise of the Eucharist, the "Bread from Heaven": "I am the bread of life; he that cometh to me shall not hunger: and he that believeth in me shall never thirst" (35). "I am the living bread which came down from heaven. If any man eat of this bread, he shall live forever; and the bread that I will give, is my flesh, for the life of the world" (51–52). "He that eateth my flesh, and drinketh my blood, abideth in me, and I in him" (57). And a year later, at the Last Supper, when He took bread and blessed it, and said, "This is my body," that tremendous promise was fulfilled, and prosy, daily bread was glorified into the "Bread of Angels."

"And I dispose to you, as my Father hath disposed to me, a kingdom; that you may eat and drink at my table in my kingdom" (Luke 22:29–30).

And just here is the point. All these glories of the Kingdom of Heaven were promised on the condition of charity. The bread of eternal life would be given only to those who would give bread to the hungry. "Come, ye blessed of my Father, possess you the Kingdom prepared for you from the foundation of the world. For I was hungry and you gave me to eat — as long as you did it to one of these my least brethren, you did it to me." Feed your neighbor, and you feed God!

We have already seen, in discussing the general giving of alms, how this command to aid the poor runs all through the teaching of the Apostles. St. Paul, the special apostle of charity, is forever dealing with the subject in a practical manner. He never ate any man's bread, but labored night and day at his tent making, so as not to be a burden to anyone. It was not a cheap pride. He did not need the help of anyone; but just the same, because he had a financial independence and had no ax to grind, he was always urging kindness, help, to others less fortunate than he. St. James, too, was a practical charity worker. He did not believe in too soft words even while he excoriated the sins of the tongue. He said: "And if a brother or a sister be naked and in want of daily food, and one of you say to them: 'Go in peace, be warmed and filled,' yet you do not give them what is necessary for the body, what does it profit? So, faith, too, unless it has works, is dead in itself" (2:14). We recall the taunt of the Saint-Simonians to Ozanam and his friends: "Show us your works!" And finally St. John in his Apocalypse recounts among the blessings of the saved that "They shall no more hunger nor thirst" (7:16).

In the lives of the saints there are many references to bread, to the feeding of the hungry. It is a common thing to read in the lives of the Fathers of the Desert that they were fed by ravens or by other miraculous means. St. Mary of Egypt, for example, lived for forty-seven years in the desert, yet the three loaves she had brought with her continued to feed her. It was the widow's cruise over again. With all of them it was trust in the Providence of God. As St. Augustine asks: "Do you think that he who feeds Christ is not fed by Him?"

All the saints were "breakers of bread." The story is told that in the year 717 Flavius Anicius Petrus, the head of what was later the great *Frangipani* family, was, on account of his generous gifts of bread during a great scarcity of food in Rome, called "Breaker of Bread"; hence the family name. St. Francis of Assisi used to call the bread that was begged the "Bread of God," or "Bread of Angels." Once when he found one of his friars starving, he set the frugal table, and ate with him and made the other friars share the meal so as not to embarrass the hungry man, who had been the victim of unregulated penance. At another time he took a hungry friar into the vineyard and ate grapes with him. "Charity is kind." To St. Francis, Lady Poverty was also Lady Courtesy. He himself went begging on the great feasts. He said that in the holy poor was fulfilled the prophecy: "Man did eat Angels' food." We are apt to think of Francis as loving only personal poverty. He loved the poor as well. And that kindness he extended even to animals. To him, "to feed the hungry" meant also to feed the animals. Speaking of Christmas, the feast he loved so well, he said: "If I knew the Emperor, I would ask him that all would be ordered on this day to throw out corn to the birds, especially to our sisters the larks, and that everyone who has a beast in the stable should give them a specially good feed for love of the Child Jesus born in a manger. And this day the rich should feed all the poor." Francis would even remove worms from the road so as to prevent their being trampled on. We recall the poet's condemnation of the man,

> Who needlessly sets foot upon a worm.

Francis loved all the works of God —

> All things both great and small.

Coleridge's "Rime of the Ancient Mariner" is a Franciscan commentary.

A book could be written on the saints' love for animals. I always feel that the writer of the Book of Tobias understood and loved animals. What a true picture he draws of the little dog. "Then the dog, which had been with them in the way, ran before, and coming *as if he had brought the news,* showed his joy by his fawning and wagging his tail" (11:9).

The old pagans punished cruelty to birds and beasts, not to vindicate them, but to condemn a vice which might be a danger to the community. The Christian was kind to animals because animals were creatures of God. The great Leonardo da Vinci used to buy birds in cages in order to set them free. Pope Pius V declared that attendance at a bullfight was incompatible with the mercy of a Christian, and that whoever fell in such combats should be buried like the beasts they had tormented. When St. Mamertinus tended the cattle the birds used to come and feed out of his hand. Once a boar sought refuge in his cell and he shielded it from pursuing dogs. St. Columban was like St. Francis in his tenderness to animals. The birds came to him and the squirrels would hide in his cowl.

If the saints could be so tender to animals, what must have been their bigness of heart in feeding the poor, since they recognized that in doing so they were feeding Christ? In that, they are the glory of the Church. "Breaker of Bread" could be the motto of any saint, as it was the motto of Christ. St. Catherine of Siena, baking bread for all the family; St. Elizabeth of Hungary carrying bread to the poor and when challenged her apron was found full of miraculous roses; Margaret Haughery feeding all the poor children of New Orleans; the countless priests and brothers and sisters breaking the bread of charity in orphanages, asylums, hospitals, and at the same time breaking the bread of life — all are the exact fulfillment of our Lord's glorification of feeding the hungry: "Come ye blessed; I was hungry and you gave me to eat."

Mother, who sang: "He hath filled the hungry," pray for us!

Chapter VI

To Give Drink to the Thirsty

IN THE Orient there is nothing of more importance than water. Explorers, excavators in Bible lands today tell us that to reconstruct the past, not only must the topography be examined, but, above all, the water resources of the site. In many places water was so scarce that when a well was dug it became a center of civilization. So today the surest sign of an historic spot, from which all other indications have disappeared, is the presence of water. The village well of Nazareth, for instance, is the same now as it was in our Lady's day. The Bedouins of the present day are full of hospitality. They would have died out long ago, save for that traditional hospitality, not from hunger but from thirst. It makes us understand why in olden times battles were fought over the possession of a well. In the Book of Genesis there are many references to wells, so absolutely necessary to the nomadic life. For purposes of cleansing as well as drinking, water had to be a prime consideration. This was especially so in those arid countries of the East where the bare feet gathered dust so quickly. One of the great acts of hospitality was to provide opportunity for the washing of the traveler's feet; an ordinary act of hospitality which in time took on the aspect of a religious rite, glorified later by our Lord when at the Last Supper He washed the feet of His apostles.

When the three visitors came to Abraham at the door

of his tent, his greeting to them was: "I will fetch a little water, and wash ye your feet" (Gen. 18:4–5). But it was for the refreshment of the body in the quenching of thirst that the scarce water was so highly prized. It was, of course, absolutely essential to life. The story of Rebecca at the well, when she replied to the servant of Isaac asking for a drink, "Drink, my lord . . . I will draw water for thy camels also" (Gen. 24:18–19), is one of the most beautiful idylls in all literature.

Water gave occasion for the Lord to work astounding miracles to provide water for the Israelites in their wandering in the desert. The waters of Mara were bitter. The Lord showed Moses a tree, and when he had cast it into the waters they were turned into sweetness (Exod. 15:25). Again, when the hand of Moses struck the rock, water spouted forth; and the Lord said, "Gather the people together, and I will give them water" (Num. 21:16).

When Balaam prophesied about Israel he conveyed his message under the figure of the precious water: "Water shall flow out of his bucket, and his seed shall be in many waters" (Num. 24:7).

In the days of Eliseus, when there was a great drought, the Lord said to him, "Make the channel of this torrent full of ditches. For thus saith the Lord: You shall not see wind nor rain: and yet this channel shall be filled with waters, and you shall drink, you and your families and your beasts" (4 Kings 3:17).

So the Psalmist, great poet that he was, saw the beauty of the waters, and their inner significance. "The Lord is upon many waters" (28:3). "He struck the rock in the wilderness, and gave them to drink, as out of the great deep. He brought forth water out of the rock: and made streams run down as rivers. . . . Because he struck the rock, and the waters gushed out, and the streams overflowed. Can he also give bread or provide a table for his people? . . . And he had commanded the clouds from above and had opened the doors of heaven. And had rained down manna upon them to eat, and had given them the bread of heaven. Man ate the bread of angels: he sent them provisions in abundance" (Ps. 77:15–25). God's displeasure was expressed in part when, "He turned their rivers into blood, and their showers that they might not drink" (Ps. 77:44), while in delivering his people he is described as the God of Jacob "Who turned the rocks into pools of water, and the stony hills into fountains of water" (Ps. 113:8).

Ecclesiasticus uses the simile of water as compared with alms: "Water quencheth a flaming fire, and alms resisteth sins" (2:33). Finally, Isaias, too, points a spiritual lesson with water: "All you that thirst come to the waters: and you that have no money, buy and eat. Come ye, buy wine and milk without money, and without any price" (55:1). "The needy and the poor seek for waters, and there are none: their tongue hath been dry with thirst" (41:17).

It is not strange, then, that in the Gospels, our Lord takes this common need of water, and, while commanding literally the giving of drink to the thirsty, also uses it to convey a spiritual message. "Whoever gives to one of these little ones but a cup of cold water to drink because he is a disciple, amen I say to you, he shall not lose his reward" (Matt. 10:42). St. Mark amplifies this by adding: "because you are Christ's" (9:40).

Water was the occasion of our Lord's first miracle, when at Cana he changed water into wine — *"The modest water saw its God and blushed."* St. Francis would have loved that. But never was fulfilled the command to give drink to the thirsty as in the sublime sermon Christ drew from water for the Samaritan woman at the Well of Jacob. "Give me to drink," He said. "If thou didst know the gift of God, and who he is that saith to thee, Give me to drink; thou perhaps wouldst have asked of him, and he would have given thee living water. . . . Whosoever drinketh of this water, shall thirst again, but he that shall drink of the water that I will give, shall not thirst forever. But the water that I will give him, shall become in him a fountain of water, springing up into life everlasting" (John 4:8–15).

Did Jesus think of the Samaritan woman when He said, "Come ye blessed. . . . I was thirsty and you gave me to drink"? Again, did He give a thought to her when He told His parable of the Good Samaritan? To give drink to the Son of God!

Later, in the temple, He cried out: "If anyone thirst, let him come to me and drink" (John 7:37).

In the Agony in the Garden He again used the figure of drink: "Father, if it is possible, let this cup pass away from me" (Matt. 26:39). Nevertheless He drained the Cup. What a drink God gave His thirsting Son!

Even when He was on the cross and His executioners offered Him wine and gall to deaden His senses, He refused. He was thirsty, even in the physical sense. "I thirst." But great as was the physical distress, His thirst was more a spiritual thirst for the souls of men and the glory of God. How thrilled any of us would be to give a cup of water to the Crucified Jesus! And yet He tells us that we accomplish the same work of mercy when we give only a drink of water to our needy neighbor. Water is such a cheap thing, a common thing. Yet that may be why our Lord delights in referring to it so often, to show us how easy it is to learn the little lesson of love.

St. John in the *Apocalypse* uses the figure of water and thirst almost as often as our Lord used it. He says of the Son of Man: "His voice like the voice of many waters" (1:16). And He that sat on the throne said: "To him who thirsts I will give of the water of life freely" (21:6). He says of the blessed: "These are they who have come out of the great tribulation, and have washed their robes and made them white in the blood of the Lamb" (7:14). "And he showed me a river of the water of life, clear as crystal, coming forth from the throne of God and of the Lamb" (22:1). I like to think that when St. John was drawing this picture of everlasting blessedness, he was thinking of the words of Jesus, "Come ye blessed. . . . I was thirsty and you gave me to drink."

It is a very striking thing, the appeal which water had to so many saints. It played a great part in the life of St. Francis. To deprive himself of it was one of his greatest penances. He would not drink, even when parched with thirst. It was the memory of our Lord's thirst on the cross; perhaps, too, in sympathy with those poor for whom Christ's mercy appealed. We recall, in his *Song to the Sun*, "Sister Water."

She most useful is, and humble, precious and pure.

It took more than a poet to choose those qualifications of water; it took a saint, seeing things through the eyes of Christ. He loved water because it symbolized the sacred penitence by which the soul is purified, and because Baptism is effected through water. He had such a great reverence for water that when he washed his hands, he turned in such a way that the drops that fell could not be trodden under foot. When he was on the way to La-Verna, where he was to receive the Stigmata, he met a peasant. The peasant gasped, "I die of thirst, for if I do not get water to drink I shall choke." Francis knelt and prayed. It would be no false interpretation to think that in that moment he thought of our Lord's command to give drink to the thirsty. At once he said to the peasant: "Hasten! Go quickly to that rock there, and you will find there running water which Jesus Christ in this hour has, in His mercy, made to issue from that rock." Immediately a spring gushed forth, and the peasant drank. The story goes on that the spring was never seen after that.

One of the followers of Francis, Brother Giles, was

carrying a jug of water along the Appian Way to Rome. A chance traveler asked him for a drink, but to the man's amazement Brother Giles refused. It seemed a queer way for the friar to keep the works of mercy. But he had his plans. As soon as he arrived at his convent, he got another jug, filled it with water, and hurried after the man he had refused. "Do not be angry with me," he said, "but I did not like to take to the monks water that another had tasted of." The true Franciscan loved Lady Courtesy.

St. Clare was so impressed with the significance of holy water as a symbol of the Blood of Christ, that she sprinkled the sisters with it all one day and exhorted them never to forget the rivers of salvation that flowed from the wounds of Christ. It is told of St. Elizabeth of Hungary that she always gave drink to the thirsty; and the drink was not always water. Once she gave beer to the poor, and the story is that the jug always remained full. St. Catherine of Siena delighted in water. "Be a vase," she said, "which you fill at the source and at the source you drink from." Once our Lord in speaking to her called Himself "The Sea Pacific."

But no saint loved water as much as St. Teresa loved it. She got many a lesson as she meditated upon it. "I love this element so much," she said, "that I have studied it more attentively than other things." She had a special confidence in Holy Water and used it continually. The Little Flower, too, saint and poet that she was, delighted in water. One needs only recall the holy wells of Ireland to know what power God is sometimes pleased to give this element. The great spot in all the world, of course, is Lourdes, where countless miracles have been wrought by the waters which our Lady discovered for St. Bernadette. It is surely a striking thing that so many of the corporal and spiritual works of mercy have been done through the water of Lourdes by Him who commanded us to give drink to the thirsty.

The Church, in the blessing of the Baptismal water, sums up all the great Scriptural references to water. "I exorcise thee, creature of water, by the living God, by the true God, by the Holy God, by the God who in the beginning by a word separated thee from the dry land: whose Spirit was borne over thee, who ordered thee to flow from Paradise, and in four rivers ordered thee to water the whole earth; who, in the desert, by the wood made thee sweet and drinkable; who produced thee from the rock, that He might refresh the people whom He had freed from Egypt, wearied with thirst. I exorcise thee by Jesus Christ, His only Son, Our Lord: who by His power converted thee at Cana of Galilee, by an admirable sign into wine; who walked upon thee, and by John in the Jordan was baptized in thee: who produced thee together with His Blood from His side; and commanded His disciples that believing they should baptize in thee." And with like solemnity is blessed the ordinary Holy Water. The blessing of the font on Holy Saturday has the same Scriptural references to water, calling it, "this holy and innocent creature." Perhaps it was here that St. Francis found his inspiration for Sister Water, "humble, precious, and pure." In the Mass, as the priest pours a little water into the chalice to be mixed with the wine, a high spiritual significance is given to it: "God, who wonderfully established the dignity of human substance, and more wonderfully reformed it, grant to us by the mystery of this water and wine, to be sharers in the Divinity of Him who deigned to participate in our humanity, Jesus Christ, Thy Son, our Lord." Reading this sublime prayer, I like to think that when our Lord made a special reference to the blessedness of giving drink to the thirsty, He was thinking of all the blessings He would give to assuage the thirst of men, even by the gift of His own Precious Blood.

It is hard for us in daily life to see why our Lord made

special mention of giving drink to the thirsty as a work of mercy. True, we have all been distressed by thirst. But at most it has been a temporary discomfort. Few ever suffer the agony of dying from lack of water. But it is a consoling thought that Christ has put the eternal premium on the simple gift of a cup of water.

Mother, "who gavest nurture from thy breast to God," pray for us!

Chapter VII

To Clothe the Naked

WHEN our Lord declared the blessedness of clothing the naked — "Come ye blessed . . . for I was naked and you clothed me" — perhaps He thought of the coming Calvary, when the executing soldiers would strip Him of His garments, and then gamble them away. Perhaps He thought, too, that His Mother had performed that corporal work of mercy when she wove for Him that seamless robe, now, alas, to furnish sport and to be given to a stranger on the throw of the dice. There is a beautiful legend that when the soldiers took away His garments our Lady gave her wimple to serve as a loin cloth for Him. She would clothe Him — the naked one — even to the end. The Son of God had "emptied" Himself, He had impoverished Himself even to the loss of His garments. Henceforth no one would clothe Him save with a winding-sheet. Nicodemus and Joseph of Arimathea, up to then comparative strangers, clothed Him with a linen shroud. "I was a stranger and you took me in." Joseph was blessed for his corporal work of mercy, even though the shelter he gave his Lord was only a tomb. He had bought the fine linen and Nicodemus added the "mixture of myrrh and aloes." They took, therefore, the body of Jesus, we are told by St. John, "and bound it in linen cloths, with the spices, as the manner of the Jews is to bury" (19:40).

Well may the words of the Sermon on the Mount here

67

come to our mind: "Be not solicitous . . . for your body, what you shall put on . . . is not the body more than the raiment? And for raiment why are you solicitous? Consider the lilies of the field, how they grow: they labor not, neither do they spin. But I say to you, that not even Solomon in all his glory was arrayed as one of these. And if the grass of the field, which is today, and tomorrow is cast into the oven, God doth so clothe: how much more you, O ye of little faith. Be not solicitous therefore, saying . . . wherewith shall we be clothed?" (Matt. 6:25, 28–31.)

The scene on Calvary where Jesus was stripped of His garments was to atone for the one in the Garden of Eden, when Adam and Eve, upon their sin, suddenly beheld their physical and moral nakedness. The poor garments which they hastily and with trembling fingers made of fig leaves was the beginning of man's clothing, a poor exchange for the shining garments of grace which they had cast off. "And the Lord God made for Adam and his wife garments of skins, and clothed them" (Gen. 3:21). God will clothe us with mercy, if in mercy we will clothe our neighbor. "I was naked and you covered me."

Clothes do not make the man — a simple truth that has become an adage. That, too, is a commentary on the Sermon on the Mount. Clothes, indeed, are of the least importance to man, even though in the growth of civilization, he, and especially she, has cultivated their fabric and style to an over importance. "Fine feathers make fine birds," is the pith of a world-old fable. That fable, too, is a commentary, but in reverse, on the Sermon on the Mount. Why, indeed, be so solicitous for peacock feathers? The only essential clothing is that which is enough to cover nakedness with decency and a sack or blanket to keep out the wintry cold. Clothes are in a far lower rank of necessities than food and drink, and none of them is as essential as cheap air which we never notice until it is vitiated by carbon monoxide. Nakedness is man's estate in the begin-

ning and at the end. As Job declared — "Naked came I
out of my mother's womb and naked shall I return thither"
(Job 1:21). From mother earth to mother earth, from
swaddling-clothes to swaddling-clothes, with but a few
changes of costumes between.

But charity covers more than nakedness; it covers a
multitude of sins. The Heart of Christ is a good place to
store the raiment of our soul where no moth can consume. To put our money into the purchase of clothes for
our needy neighbor is a good way to invest for the obtain-
ing of our own Easter rig, or for our own eternal wedding
garment. Somehow, when I think of the white robes of the
blessed in heaven, robes woven on the looms of Paradise,
and "made white in the blood of the Lamb," I have the
vision described in Tennyson's *Idylls of the King* when
Sir Belvidere threw the sword Excalibur into the mire and
it was grasped by an arm

Clothed in white samite, mystic, wonderful.

It is striking, in the Apocalypse, to find how often St.
John describes the clothing of the saints. Was he remem-
bering how his Master ordered him to clothe the naked?

Granted that clothing is in itself essentially unim-
portant, that in some climes it is even a burden, yet
among civilized peoples, apart from any artistic purpose,
it has become a prime essential for the very preservation
of life. And proper, decent clothing. You cannot expect
people to go about in sacks or blankets, though even that
style would be more becoming to Christians than the
immodest clothes some of them affect. But decent clothes
are necessary. Hence the law of God has dealt with that
necessity, and has put its sanction upon the right of man
to be granted decent, becoming attire. The Providence of
God in providing that covering is evident in the beginning. Moses declares that God "doth judgment to the
fatherless and the widows, loveth the stranger and giveth

him food and raiment" (Deut. 10:18). The law had been given in Exodus: "If thou take of thy neighbor a garment in pledge, thou shalt give it him again before sunset" (22:25). And it is added later "that he may sleep in his own garment" (Deut. 24:13). This is an illuminating point since the oriental dress served not only for covering of the body by day, but also for covering by night. It helps us to understand why our Lord made it a special work of mercy — to clothe the naked.

Job in his humble charity takes glory in the fact that he had clothed the poor: "If I have despised him that was perishing for want of clothing and the poor man that had no covering; if his sides have not blessed me, and if he were not warmed with the fleece of my sheep . . . let my shoulder fall from its joint, and let my arm with its bones be broken" (Job 31:19–22).

In the beautiful tribute to the valiant woman, much is made of her zeal in providing clothing: "She hath sought wool and flax, and hath wrought by the counsel of her hands . . . she hath opened her hand to the needy, and stretched out her hands to the poor. She shall not fear for her house in the cold of the snow: for all her domestics are clothed with double garments" (Prov. 31:13, 20–21). It sounds like a description of the queenly housewife, St. Elizabeth of Hungary.

The prophet Ezechiel proclaims a blessing on the man who aids the poor: "he hath given his bread to the hungry, and covered the naked with a garment" (18:7).

But it is in the New Testament that this duty of clothing the poor receives its greatest beatitude. There are, it is true, not so many specific references to clothing the naked as, for instance, to feeding the hungry, but, of course, all the commands to general almsgiving include this particular manifestation of charity. Yet, as we have seen, our Lord uses the idea of raiment to point one of His most beautiful lessons about the Providence of God, in telling His

hearers to consider the lilies and the grass of the field.
Yet He did not leave it all to an idle trust in God's Providence, or perhaps He wished to impress upon them that
He would have that Providence act through the charity
of the souls He would win to His Gospel. For, as we have
seen in regard to other works of mercy, He made essential
to salvation the compliance with the obligation to clothe
the naked: "Come ye blessed . . . [I was] naked and you
covered me. Depart from me, you cursed . . . [I was]
naked and you covered me not" (Matt. 25).

Even before our Lord began to preach, St. John the
Baptist, as we have seen, had insisted with his disciples
and followers upon the duty of charity. He did not overlook the act of clothing of the naked. "Let him who has
two tunics share with him who has none; and let him
who has food do likewise." John was true to the glorious
line of prophets in his concern for the poor.

You will not find in the apostles many references to
the duty of providing the poor with clothing. Again, that
was one department of the practical duty of almsgiving,
and it was not neglected any more than the providing of
food and drink and all the other needs of man. There is
a lovely incident narrated in the *Acts*. In Joppe there
was a disciple named Tabitha, or Dorcas, "full of good
works and alms deeds." She died; and her friends sent
for Peter who happened to be in the near-by town of
Lydda. Peter came, and they brought him into where
the dead woman lay. "And all the widows stood about
him weeping, and showing him the coats and garments
which Dorcas made them." Peter prayed, and restored
her to life. Was it not, perhaps, because Dorcas had been
a seamstress for the poor? "I was naked, and you covered
me."

Since our Lord insisted upon the specific duty of
clothing the naked, there must have been some particular
reason. Our Lord never wasted words. The reason may

be put down as His wish to convince us that the needs of the whole man, corporal and spiritual, must be provided for. It was not enough to give a man a bit to eat and a drop to drink. He was to be treated as a civilized being, a social being, to whom social justice must be done. That thought is paramount in the Encyclical of Pius XI, *Atheistic Communism*. He says there: "But social justice cannot be said to have been satisfied as long as working-men are denied a salary that will enable them to secure proper sustenance for themselves and for their families; as long as they are denied the opportunity of acquiring a modest fortune and forestalling the plague of universal pauperism, as long as they cannot make suitable provision, through public or private insurance for old age, for periods of illness and unemployment."

Clothes do not make the man, but they are a great help to his self-respect. And it would be an act lacking in full charity to fill his stomach and let him go in rags. It should be simple enough to provide all men with the common decencies of life.

The true Christian does not require royal raiment. He is not "a man clothed in soft garments." As our Lord said of John the Baptist, "Behold they that are in costly apparel and live delicately, are in the houses of kings." But the ordinary man, when left to himself and free from the foolish pride of trying to keep up with the flashy neighbors, is content with simple things. He is not keen about fine feathers. He is happiest in the minimum of clothing. St. Paul sensed that, and he urged a simple life. Said he, "For we brought nothing into the world, and certainly we can take nothing out: but having food, and sufficient clothing let us be content" (1 Tim. 6:7–9). In so many words St. Paul coined the slogan — "You can't take it with you." "We can take nothing out." Our only raiment at the end will be a shroud, and it will not be much of a style show with only the worms to see it. The worms in the grave must laugh at the precious threads their silkworm cousins once wove. It makes little difference, however, of what material our shroud will be made. We are weavers of a spiritual fabric; or, rather, it is being woven by the fingers of the naked neighbor whom we cover.

There is a beautiful contrast pictured in the Scriptures in regard to our Lady, the Mother of Mercy. The Gospel tells how when Jesus was born she wrapped Him in swaddling-clothes and laid Him in a manger. "I was naked and you clothed me." His Mother was the first to do unto Him this corporal work of mercy. The years passed during which she made His garments. And then at the end, as described in the Apocalypse, she shines forth as the "woman clothed with the sun." "Come ye blessed!" But most of all His Blessed Mother, as He remembered the baby clothes of her making.

In the lives of the saints there is hardly a work of mercy that shines with so much spiritual poetry as this one, of clothing the naked. It pointed the charity sermons of the Fathers. So St. Cyprian exclaimed: "Let us give to Jesus Christ the vestments of earth, to receive from Him the vestments of heaven."

The most famous legend of all is that concerning St. Martin of Tours. One day — he was only a catechumen at the time — he cut his cloak in two and gave half of it to a beggar. Lo and behold, the following night he had a vision in which he saw Christ wearing that half. Our Lord said to him: "Martin, while yet a catechumen, has clothed me with this garment." It is related that the Kings of France used to carry into battle the cloak of St. Martin. Those who carried the cloak, in Latin *cappa*, were called Cappelani, or cloak-bearers, and hence the term chaplain.

St. Felix of Nola gave to the poor everything he could lay his hands on. If he happened to have two coats — that rarely happened — he gave away the better one, and often exchanged his only one for the rags of a beggar. It has ever been the conviction of the saints that if they slighted a beggar, it was probable that they were slighting Christ under the guise of a beggar. It was more than a probability; it was a certainty, since Christ in detailing the works of mercy insisted that what we do for them we do for Him.

A humorous but edifying story is told of St. John the Almoner, a nobleman of the sixth century, who called the poor his "lords and masters." In his youth he had had a vision of a beautiful maiden crowned with olive who told him that she was Compassion, eldest daughter of the Great King. He, too, gave to the poor all he could lay his hands on. Anyway, the story goes that a rich man gave him a valuable blanket. The very next morning John sold the blanket and gave the proceeds to his poor. The rich man bought him a second, and a third blanket, and so on and on, but every time John sold the blanket for the poor, as he laughingly said, "We shall see who will be tired first!" I imagine it was the rich man.

But it was especially the Franciscan idea to clothe the poor. St. Francis did not care much about clothes for himself, a sack and a rope, that was enough. He had seen too much of the folly of dress when he was a gay young blade, the son of a cloth merchant.

Once he was asked how he could bear the cold with such scanty clothing. He replied: "If through our yearning for the heavenly fatherland we have been inwardly kindled by the flame, we can easily endure this bodily cold." Yet severe as he was with himself, he did not ask the poor to take his own bitter medicine. Rather was he solicitous for their comfort. Once when he was given a cloak, he said: "We ought to return this cloak to its owner, for we received it only as a loan, until we should come upon one poorer than ourselves." And again: "I will not be a thief. For it would be counted to us for a theft if we should not give to him who is more needy." The life of Francis seemed to have much to do with giving away cloaks. He was like St. John the Almoner and his blankets. One day an old woman asked Francis for an alms. He gave her his cloak. She immediately cut it up, but it was not enough to make her a dress. So back she went to Francis to beg more cloth. Francis did not order her away, but he asked one of his friars to part with his cloak, to help the old woman dress herself up.

It was the same spirit with all his companions. The famous Brother Giles once met a poor man, and was struck with pity at his scanty clothing. Giles had only one tunic, so he gave his hood to the man. He went hoodless for twenty days, suffering much from the cold. But his heart was warm. Brother Juniper, the simple friar, whom St. Clare called "the plaything of God," gave away his tunic so many times that he was finally forbidden to do so. But he got around it some way. One day he met a beggar, and said to him: "My superior has forbidden me to give away my tunic, but if you take it from me I will not stop you." He was not so simple after all. In our common parlance, it is the greatest tribute to a man's generosity to say that he would give you his shirt. Common expression though it is, it describes perfectly the Franciscan practice. It was always a Franciscan trait to clothe the poor. St. Elizabeth of Hungary was always making clothes for the poor, from the cradle to the grave. She would strip her beds of the sheets to make shrouds for the neglected dead.

But of all the saints, I always think of St. Catherine of Siena when there is talk of clothing the poor. She even parted with her cloak. She was severely reprimanded for this, and was reminded that only bad women went out on the street without a cloak. "Never mind," she said, "I would rather go without a cloak than without charity."

It was her solid interpretation of the text: "charity covereth a multitude." Better to let the pharisees be scandalized than make the poor suffer.

There is a story told of Catherine which no doubt she herself laughed at, for she had a fine sense of humor. Her father had given her permission to take anything she wanted for her poor. He must have winced a bit when she gave away a whole hogshead of wine. It was all right with the father, but all the other members of the family had to lock their cupboards or Catherine would not have left them a stitch to put on. One day Catherine saw from her window a poor man lying in the street. He was half naked. She got a loaf of bread and carried it out and put it beside him. When he came to, he asked her for some cast-off clothes, too. So at once she gave him her cloak. That night our Lord appeared to her and said: "Daughter, thou hast clothed and covered my nakedness. I will therefore now clothe thee with the fulness of my grace." It is said that from that moment she never felt cold, no matter how lightly she was clad. A final story about her: One day in church a beggar who was perishing from the cold asked her for an alms. She might have laughed, for she did not have a cent. But rather than refuse the beggar, she asked one of the women with her to cut a piece from her sleeveless tunic. Catherine gave the piece of cloth to the poor man. He was not satisfied, and asked for more, at least a rag of a shirt. So Catherine went home and got him a shirt. Again he asked for more, and Catherine gave him the sleeves of a shirt belonging to her brother. The next day a man met her, and said to her: "Catherine, do you recognize me?" Then he suddenly disappeared, and Catherine knew that it was the Lord.

Legends, some may say. But there is a Gospel truth beneath them all. These sudden appearances of Christ in the guise of a beggar are His way to give occasion to His saints to do the works of mercy so dear to Him. But somehow we do not need these miraculous visions to give us opportunities to clothe the naked. Our opportunities are not as dramatic. They are rather prosy, even humdrum. To make clothes for poor children; to help the sisters who run our orphanages; to give money to the Holy Childhood to clothe abandoned babies; to make altar linens for the missions, swaddling clothes, as it were, for the Babe of Bethlehem; to knit socks and sweaters for our servicemen; there are countless ways in which we can respond to the appeal of Christ to clothe the naked. It may not seem much. We forget the gifts as soon as they are made. But Christ will never forget them. No moth will ever consume them. They will be like His garments at the Transfiguration — "and His garments became white as snow."

Nothing is ever lost that is given to God, and "inasmuch as ye have done it to these my least brethren ye have done it unto me."

Mother of Mercy, "Clothed with the sun," pray for us!

Chapter VIII

To Ransom the Captive

CHILDREN studying the Catechism are rather non-plussed about the work of mercy — to ransom the captive. Perhaps they understand the phrase better today, when there are so many prisoners of war. But when we were children there were within our ken no such beings as captives. Perhaps if they had said "to free the slaves" we should have grasped it better, so close were we to the Civil War and Lincoln.

Yet for centuries there was in Christendom no more urgent need than the redemption of captives and the freeing of slaves. For servitude was a necessary consequence of barbarism.

It is quite impossible to trace slavery to its beginnings. It seems to have existed in the world always. Such an inhuman thing could have originated only in a barbarism which believed that might was right. There was evidently no conception of the equality of man. In early times of paganism, when weak women and children received absolutely no consideration, if support was not got by marriage, the only alternative was to get it by selling oneself. Slavery could be the only provision when relatives failed.

So from a very early age, society was divided into citizens and slaves; the slaves forming by far the greater part. Thus we are told that in Attica in the fourth century B.C. four hundred thousand out of five hundred thousand were slaves. Slavery was, indeed an integral part of Greek civilization. The more intellectual the people became, the more slavery increased. It was the belief that some races are by nature superior — the Nazi complex of our own day — and others just born to be slaves. Naturally there had to be some kind of provision made for the slaves; hence there was a species of brotherhood of owners and slaves, not, indeed, for the welfare of the slaves but for civic betterment and for financial reasons. The slave was not considered a person. Aristotle, for instance, held that slavery was natural and even necessary. Plato considered slaves as only half men, a kind of superior animal. Galen speaks of the usefulness of dissecting slaves, and in Rome it was the custom to perform autopsies on slaves alone. So Rome regarded slavery as essential. The war captives, amounting to hundreds of thousands in the great days of Roman conquest, were sold into slavery. Many, too, were brought by pirates from all parts of the Empire. More than that, a father could legally sell his own children.

And the slaves were not all of inferior mental ability. They were not even all manual laborers. Artists, actors, professors, secretaries, copyists and holders of "white-collar" jobs were among the slaves. In Italy, in the time of the Emperor Claudius, there were over twenty million slaves, at least as many slaves as freemen, although some historians say that the slaves outnumbered the free three to one. It was not a healthy condition for any state. Slavery was a prime cause of poverty and degradation, for slave labor crushed free labor, and by degrees the slaves practically dispossessed the freemen. It is well to remember these facts as the background for the preaching of Christianity with its insistence upon the dignity of the human soul.

The owner of a slave had absolute dominion over him, he could kill him or let him live. Sick slaves were cast out as of no commercial value. Every slave had to wear chains, as the badge of servitude. But finally the slaves became so numerous that they constituted a menace to their masters. There were, indeed, from time to time serious insurrections, and as a result many slaves were freed. It seemed that they never appreciated their full power, or they could have overthrown the Empire. It is necessary to get this background, necessary to understand how slavery vitiated all Roman life. Only by appreciating its horrors and its dangers to civilization can you understand the supreme importance of Christ's command regarding the captive: "I was in prison and you visited me."

Far different from Greece and Rome, the Mosaic Law, while tolerating servitude, but not approving it, commanded that mercy be shown to the slave. There is no need to study all the texts. There was no such degradation among the Jews as among the Greeks and Romans. Mercy was forever preached, though a mercy far below the quality of the mercy of Christianity. The wonderful law of jubilee freed the Hebrew slave and his children. The reason for the mercy is given over and over again: "Remember that thou wast a servant in Egypt." The Jews never forgot that Joseph had been an Egyptian slave.

The establishment of certain cities of refuge to which accused criminals could flee for safety indicates the great mercy of the Mosaic Law. The entire chapter XX of the Book of Josue deals with these cities of refuge. It was, like the jubilee, a unique institution. The right of finding sanctuary at the altar, which was so important later on in Christianity, was a common one with the Jews. They never forgot their own servitude. So, one of the great Messianic prophecies of Isaias was in regard to slaves. "He hath sent me . . . to preach a release to the captives and deliverance to them that are shut up" (61:1). So, too, Jeremias declared: "Thus saith the Lord: Execute judgment and justice and deliver him that is oppressed" (22:3). All in all, it is a high appreciation of mercy. How could it be otherwise, since it is the word of God.

But it is in the New Testament that the redemption of the captive takes on a new meaning. Jesus preached, "Blessed are you when men persecute you." He Himself was a captive. He was imprisoned before His Crucifixion; He was made a lower criminal than Barabbas, who was released in His stead; His precursor, John the Baptist, was killed in prison; He preached "release to the captives; and finally as a prisoner He was nailed to the cross between two other prisoners. Beautifully has He been called the "Prisoner of Love." As Prisoner, who "led Captivity Captive," He exacted that His followers should serve a term in prison. In the *Acts* we have one incident after another of the imprisonment of the Apostles. Peter and John are imprisoned, Paul and Silas are imprisoned and scourged. Peter is bound in chains and imprisoned. Paul declares that in every city imprisonment awaits him. Felix leaves Paul in prison, again Paul is scourged and bound with straps and imprisoned, and at Rome he is guarded by a soldier. Paul is always wearing chains. His whole Apostolic life seems to consist in changing from one prison to another. He is always serving time as well as "redeeming the time." And finally at Rome he is imprisoned and beheaded, as St. Peter is nailed to the Cross. Paul was always referring to his chains: "Remember my chains," "I am an ambassador in chains," "I, Paul, the prisoner of Jesus Christ," "even to bonds, as a criminal." So, St. Paul, while spending so much of his life in chains, was in a position to advise his fellow-captives, the slaves. He was not supine. He insisted on his Roman citizenship, he insisted on the right of freedom, for all were one in Christ Jesus. "There is neither slave nor freeman" (Gal. 3:28). He was not a radical. He did not attempt to abolish slavery at one blow. He had common sense. He knew that to try to remedy the evil by rebellion and force would bring on a more terrible calamity. His idea was establish the Christian principle of brotherly love and eventually the freedom of every man will result. This thought is particularly striking in his treatment of the slave Onesimus. Paul in his first imprisonment at Rome knew the slave, who had run away from his master Philemon, a wealthy Christian of Colossae. Paul converted Onesimus, and then sent him back to Philemon, with a letter telling Philemon to receive Onesimus back, "instead of a slave as a brother most dear."

Again and again he deals with the slave question, exhorting slaves to obey their masters, to honor them, even the severe ones, "that the name of the Lord and His teaching be not blasphemed." Paul would not foster rebellion. It would have hurt the slave no less than set Christianity back. His idea was: bear with the evil for a while.

"Wast thou a slave when called? (i.e., to the faith). Let it not trouble thee. But if thou canst become free, make use of it rather. For a slave who has been called in the Lord, is a freedman of the Lord; just as a free man who has been called is a slave of Christ. You have been bought with a price; do not become the slaves of men. Brethren, in the state in which he was when called, let every man remain with God" (1 Cor. 7:21–24).

This teaching of St. Paul to the slaves was of tremendous importance to civilization. It is easy enough to say that Christianity from the start should have emancipated the slave. Had it done so, hell would have been let loose. To have started a rebellion would have been fatal. While really believing that master and slave were equal in the eyes of their Creator, the only sane thing to do was to accept conditions as they were, to go along calmly, to preach the right of freedom, equality, to sow the seed of religion and let it bear fruit in God's good time. Establish Christian principles, and the rest would follow. A sudden emancipation, indeed, would have been disastrous to the slaves themselves. So the Church went on, telling the masters and slaves of their mutual obligations, sanctifying

them with her Sacraments — in Roman law, for instance
the slave could have no legitimate marriage or paternity
— making the priests set the example of kindness, working
out all in patience. It took a long time, indeed; as late as
the seventh century slavery existed in some places. We are
not considering its revival in modern times.

The Church's stand in behalf of the slaves, who in the
early days constituted a great part of her membership,
transformed all society. The Church, after Christ and the
apostles, glorified work. Paul, and all the other apostles
supported themselves. To that degree they were like the
toiling slaves. There was scarcely more than a nominal
difference if the Spirit of the Gospel was observed. Before
Christ's preaching the slave was a *thing;* now he was a
brother of Christ the Laborer, a brother to his master in
Christ. Hence the Christian master came to regard his
slave as his brother in Christ, freed him from toil on Sun-
days and holy days, gave him the chance to marry and
lead a family life — in a word, treated him as a human
being. And the slave, no longer obeying from fear, but
from a spiritual motive, became content. He had regained
his self-respect. He could aspire even to the highest honors
in the Church. Many slaves became priests, bishops, and
some, as Pius and Callistus, became Popes! In the Christian cemeteries there was no difference — in paganism
there was — between the tombs of the slaves and the free.
The growth of the idea that every man is an individual,
free in Christ, finally ended slavery. Christianity was the
original Declaration of Independence.

Many a time the early Church redeemed slaves, and
heroic Christians sold themselves into slavery to free
others. The heroic St. Anastasia, belonging to one of the
first families of Rome, visited the Christians in prison and
gave them all she had. When they were executed she
would weep, saying that the persecutors had taken from
her the objects of her mercy. Rejected by her pagan hus-

band, she was put in prison, where she was fed for two years by heavenly manna, and at last burned alive. St. Telemachus, a solitary of the East, grieved over the killing of the gladiators, all slaves. He came to Rome, and one day rushed in among them in the amphitheater, and was torn to pieces. He truly redeemed the captives, for the Emperor Honorius as a result of the tragedy abolished the inhuman combats. The early saints, like St. Ignatius, martyr, were all used to jails. Their deaths softened the hearts of even the pagans. But the Christians were so impressed by the concern of the Church for the captives, that many of them not only freed their own slaves, but also gave away much of their property for the redemption of others. St. Melania, for example, who was fabulously rich, freed thousands of her slaves. The average price of a slave was one hundred dollars.

Where outright freedom was not feasible, the lot of the slaves was vastly bettered. Slaves were permitted to marry freemen. Jews were forbidden to keep Christian slaves; traffic in slaves was forbidden; and a free man could not be reduced to slavery. If a slave wished to become a monk, he did not need the permission of his master.

When the Church gradually became a great proprietor and inherited slaves, she freed them, if it were possible, and, if it were not feasible to do that, she bettered their condition immeasurably. She never forgot our Lord's blessing — "I was in prison and you visited me." From the beginning the Church exercised that work of mercy. When Christians were imprisoned for the faith, she ordered the faithful to visit them and comfort them both materially and spiritually, to raise money to buy their liberty, or at least to obtain the mitigation of their sufferings. This was accomplished through the Deacons and Deaconesses, since they were less suspect than the Bishops; but the chief burden was on the Bishops, who bought the captives, took up collections for them, even sold church property to free them and had the prisons inspected every Sunday, Wednesday, and Friday. Not only did they help their immediate subjects, but they contributed to the relief of prisoners in foreign lands. The ransoming of captives was always a big business with the Catholic Church. When the Church came into power, she sought to eliminate imprisonment, striving to correct it in other ways. So, eventually, at Easter all prisoners were set free, save those who were guilty of the greatest crimes. There is an interesting item in old English Church law forbidding the sale of church goods unless the money was to be used for the ransom of slaves. The Church continued to be the perennial fount of mercy. In line with that mercy was the famous right of sanctuary. If a person unjustly accused went into a church, he was safe, until such time as the courts decided his case. It was similar to the rite of asylum attached to the pagan Greek temples and altars, and to the cities of refuge, and right of sanctuary under the Mosaic Law. But it was practiced universally by the Church. The idea was eminently sane and merciful. It averted the danger of lynch-law. It is an interesting study, but it would take us too far afield here. Finally the right of sanctuary, or asylum, was so badly abused that it had to be abolished.

To return to the slaves, or captives. The Christian Emperors tried to better their condition, but "the laws of Caesar are one thing, the laws of Christ another." The laws of Caesar could not approach Christ's ideal. Even when with the invasion of the barbarians the number of slaves increased and their lot became harder, the Church insisted on lenient laws and continued to redeem war captives, sending back thousands to their native lands. She was tireless, against great odds. There are many heroic examples. St. Caesarius sold the sacred vessels to ransom prisoners of war; St. Ambrose broke and sold his for the same purpose; St. Germain, of Paris, gave away everything, even his clothes. St. Paulinus, Bishop of Nola, was so moved by the tears of a widow whose son was a prisoner that he exchanged places with him and worked as a slave gardener for an African chieftain; St. Patrick, and St. Bridget, too, had been slaves in Ireland, and wished to preserve Ireland from slavery and its evils, especially from the invasions of the pirates and the trafficking in men. It was no disgrace for the saint to be a slave, as, of course, St. Paul has proved. St. Febronia, dragged before the tribunal of the prosecutor, was asked if she were slave or free. Proudly she answered, "A slave, and the slave of Christ."

One of the best friends to the slaves was St. Gregory the Great, the first Pope to adopt the title, "Servant of the Servants of God." His declaration freeing two slaves precedes, in very similar words, the Declaration of Independence by many centuries: "Since the Redeemer and Creator of the world made Himself incarnate in the form of humanity in order to break the chains of our slavery by the grace of freedom, and to restore us to our pristine liberty, it is well and wise to restore the benefit of original liberty to men whom nature has made free, and whom the laws of men have bowed under the yoke of servitude. For this reason we make you, Montanus and Thomas, servants of the holy Roman Church, which we also serve with the help of God, free from this day and Roman citizens, and we make over to you all your stock of money."

He ordered that every pagan and Jewish slave who wished to become Christians, be redeemed at the expense of the Church. There is one particularly beautiful incident in his life. A young slave girl wished to become a nun. Gregory wrote to a subdeacon at the church of which she was a member. "I understand that the defensor Felix possesses a young woman called Catella, who seeks with tears and vehement desire to take the veil, but whose master will not permit her to assume it. Now, I want you to go to Felix, and demand of him the soul of this girl. You will pay him the price he wants, and send her here under the care of competent persons who will conduct her to a monastery. And do it at once, that your delay may not put this soul in danger."

Gregory would have solved the slave problem at once if he had had his way, but the Church suffered from Emperors who wanted to be complete masters. The saying was, "The baptized of the evening expect to be the pontiffs and doctors of the next day." The real persecutors were the sectaries, such as the Arians, who tried to divide the Church. Society to a great extent, though openly Christian, was pagan at heart, ruled by pagan laws. Unjust taxation had ruined the Roman world. No wonder that taxation and constant war reduced free men to slavery — until they were in the Empire one hundred and twenty-million slaves. Gradually the light penetrated the darkness. By the Middle Ages real slavery no longer existed in Christian lands, though there was the kindred evil of serfdom, where a man was personally free but was bound to the soil on which he worked. But even in time that serfdom also disappeared. All betterment was due to the Church, which taught that Pope and Prince must give due account to God. Indeed, it was the monks and friars who alleviated the condition of the serfs and finally abolished serfdom as well as slavery. Yet even for a while slavery was revived in some Catholic countries, as Italy and Spain, where the wars against the Turks brought war captives to Europe. Hence there was still need for the Church to preach the redemption of captives, especially in the Crusades when many fell into the hands of the infidels. Innocent III (1216) wrote to the Patriarch of Jerusalem, "whoever delivers any of the faithful from prison will be delivered by Christ from Hell."

To remedy the crying evil many religious Orders arose, just for this purpose of rescuing captives. The Order of

Calatrava, the Mercedarians, or Order of Our Lady of Mercy, or Ransom, founded by St. Peter Nolasco; the Trinitarians, founded by St. John of Matha — all these did more than their share to save Christianity. The Trinitarians in time had two hundred and fifty houses, with lay confraternities attached. It is estimated that in three hundred years they redeemed nine hundred thousand captives by money and by personal replacement. Their vow was: "To become a hostage in the hands of the infidels, if that is necessary, for the deliverance of Christ's faithful."

There was a special tenderness in the saints for captives. St. Francis of Assisi even pitied captive animals, and always tried to buy their freedom. He considered himself a captive, lodging in caves which he called "prisons." Once when a youth he had been a prisoner of war, a prisoner, too, in his father's house. When he was at Rome he would walk around the prison walls every day, and would go in to preach to the prisoners and to console them. St. Dominic offered to exchange places with a captive of the Moors, because the poor fellow had a family dependent on him.

There was no one more interested in prisoners than St. Catherine of Siena. She called them her "dearest sons in Christ Jesus," never reproaching them but urging them to be patient, as Christ was patient in suffering. Her prayer on Good Friday, among many petitions, begged God to open prisons, to loose chains. In her time many were condemned to death, and many died inpenitent. She would spend the night in prayer, and then in the morning go to the prisons to exhort to penance. She always converted them. She would accompany them to their execution. She would receive their dead bodies, happy when her white tunic was sprinkled with their blood. There is nothing in all literature more thrilling than her letter relating the death of Niccolo Tuldo, a young Sienese noble.

St. Vincent of Paul had been a slave at Algiers and had seen the sufferings of the Christian captives and the dangers to their faith. "I have seen the wretched men treated like beasts," he said. Hence when he got the power, there was no work so dear to him as the care of the galley slaves, poor convicts, to the number of four thousand, manning the oars, the most pitiful beings in all the world. When Vincent was made Chaplain of the Galleys he went heart and soul at the work of comforting them and reclaiming them spiritually. He loved the sick ones especially, and hired a house to care for them. He sent some of his priests to Africa where, besides redeeming twelve hundred captives in a few years, they converted many more and helped them at death. And he instilled the same spirit into the Sisters of Charity, who served the slaves, even while they were greeted with vile language and had the soup thrown into their faces.

St. Teresa was living in days when the ransom of captives was a practical duty. She could see on the walls of a church in Toledo thousands of chains, votive offerings of ransomed captives. She tells us of a Franciscan lay brother, whom she knew well, who wanted to exchange places with some captives. His superiors thought him mad, but finally gave him permission. Her dearest friend, Father Gracian, unjustly expelled from the Carmelites after her death, was captured by pirates and imprisoned in a dungeon for two years at Tunis. There he labored among the Christian slaves. Finally he was ransomed, and his innocence was established at Rome. Pope Clement VIII said, "This man is a saint." St. Charles Borromeo, too, loved prisoners and established a model prison system in his diocese.

But while slavery was dying out in the old world it was revived in the new, especially by the Spaniards. The Popes protested. Pius II had called slavery, "a great crime," and all tried to put it down. Las Casas fought slavery bitterly. The Dominicans refused to absolve the slave trafficker. St. Peter Claver, at Cartagena, the slave center of the world, where a thousand slaves landed every month, called himself the "Slave of Slaves," and for forty-four years ministered to them, baptizing three hundred thousand negroes.

Even to recent times slavery existed in Africa. The Popes continued to fight it. Pius IX called it the "supreme villainy." Leo XIII, encouraging the work of Cardinal Lavigeri, called it the "accursed pest," and ordered collections in every Catholic Church to fight it. Popes had long condemned slavery, before the famous words of Jefferson, about slavery: "I tremble for my country when I reflect that God is just."

It is thrilling to recall how the Church in all ages fought the evil of slavery and responded to the call of Christ. "I was in prison and you visited me." "Come ye blessed."

But still there are innumerable prisoners in the world. We may not purchase their bodies, but we may purchase their souls by our prayers.

Mother of Mercy, Help of Christians, pray for us!

Chapter IX

To Harbor the Harborless

A WRITER in the *National Geographic Magazine* of recent issue says that even today the poorest Bedouin is as gracious in his hospitality as Abraham was to the strangers whom he summoned to break bread with him. He will slaughter his last sheep to feed the visitor, and consider as an enemy anyone who will not sit in his guest tent. He shares that hospitality even with an enemy. Frugal ordinarily, he will kill the fatted sheep to entertain his guests.

It is like a page from the Old Testament, where hospitality is set forth as a Divine Command. Time and again the order is given not to molest a stranger, "for you also were strangers in the land of Egypt" (Exod. 23:9).

"Let him be among you as one of the same country: and you shall love him as yourselves" (Lev. 19:34). In the Sabbatical year the order was not to gather "the grapes of the first fruits as a vintage . . . but they shall be unto you for meat, to thee and to thy manservant, to thy maidservant, and thy hireling, and to the strangers that sojourn with thee" (Lev. 25:5–6). "Cursed be he that perverteth the judgment of the stranger" (Deut. 27:19); "thou shalt not abhor the . . . Egyptian" (23:7); and always the reason for the hospitality is given — you were once a stranger yourself in Egypt. Even the ass or ox of a neighbor was not to be let go astray.

There is one text that must have delighted St. Francis in its care of animals: "If thou findest as thou walkest by the way a bird's nest in a tree or on the ground, and the dam sitting upon the young or upon the eggs; thou shalt not take her with her young. But shalt let her go, keeping the young which thou has caught: that it may be well with thee, and thou mayst live a long time" (Deut. 22:6–7).

We are told that Tobias gave all his tithes to the proselytes and strangers (1:7). Ezechiel accuses those who have opressed the stranger in Jerusalem (22–7), and Zacharias commands: "And oppress not the widow and the fatherless, and the stranger, and the poor" (7:10).

The Jews had always been taught to exercise hospitality, even to strangers, but it was a limited hospitality. The stranger hardly included the non-Jew, for we find St. Peter saying, "You know it is not permissible for a Jew to associate with a foreigner or to visit him" (Acts 10:28). It took a miracle to convince him that non-Jews came into the scheme of salvation. Yet he had been listening to Jesus declaring the blessedness of those to whom He shall say on the last day: "I was a stranger and you took me in." And that was not a limited invitation of our Lord, "Come to me, all you who labor and are burdened, and I will give you rest" (Matt. 11:28).

In His public life He could say: "The foxes have dens, and the birds of the air have nests, but the Son of Man has nowhere to lay His head" (Luke 9:58). But, nevertheless, He accepted hospitality, even from publicans and sinners, and was condemned by the religious leaders because those who entertained Him were suspect.

There is nothing lovelier than the hospitality shown Him by Martha and Mary. Accepting hospitality, He insisted that His disciples, too, be shown hospitality. "But whatever town you enter, and they do not receive you—go out into the streets and say, 'Even the dust from your town that cleaves to us we shake off against you. Yet know this, that the Kingdom of God is at hand.' I say to you, that it

will be more tolerable for Sodom in that day than for
that town" (Luke 10:10–12). Hospitality to all was to be
a mark of Christianity. St. John, to whom was given the
honor of receiving as his guest the very Mother of God,
as he took her to his own, never ceased to urge hospitality. "Beloved, thou dost in accordance with faith whatever
thou workest for the brethren, and that even when they
are strangers" (3 John 1:5). St. Peter, too: "Be hospitable
to one another without murmuring" (1 Pet. 4:9). And St.
Paul, always preaching and practising charity, does not
forget hospitality. One of the first qualifications that he
demands of a bishop is that he must be "hospitable"
(Titus 1:9); and the "widow" must have the reputation
for "practising hospitality in washing the saints' feet" (1
Tim. 5:10). Again "Do not forget to entertain strangers,
for thereby some have entertained angels unawares" (Heb.
13:1). "Welcome him [i.e., Epaphroditus], then, with all
joy in the Lord, and show honor to men like him" (Phil.
2:29–30).

Hospitality, of course, was not solely a Jewish trait.
Even the pagan nations highly regarded it as a great virtue. This was so even among the Greeks and the Romans.
An exception should be made of the Egyptians, for they
hated foreigners. But with most of the patriarchal tribes
hospitality was absolutely necessary. In the desert there
could be no living without it. It was, however, a special
practice of the Jews, though not always from the highest
motives. Just here is the difference between ordinary,
natural hospitality and Christian hospitality — the latter is
done for the sake of Christ. "I was a stranger, and you
took me in."

Among the Jews, however, hospitality often had a religious motive. For example, in the Greek Dispersion of the
Jews there was a religious sanction for hospitality of Jew
for Jew. The Talmud has it: "Whoever receives under his
roof a disciple or a learned man, giving him food and

drink, and bestowing goods upon him, does the same as if he offered a daily sacrifice." But Christianity took the natural virtue of hospitality and glorified it. Receive your neighbor, and you receive God. Receive your neighbor as you would receive Christ. That beautiful idea of Christian hospitality is expressed over and over in the writings of the Fathers, in practically the same words: "Let every Christian have a hospice in his own home, a house into which Christ may enter. Say, 'This is Christ's room.' " As St. Peter Chrysologus puts it, "Give a roof and receive Heaven."

In every inn, in the Middle Ages, there were holy images in the guest rooms. There was a room, or at least a table, even for the excommunicated. More, the stranger was welcomed in the humblest cottage, for to refuse the stranger was to refuse Christ.

We read of the great Pope, St. Leo, who, thinking he had slighted a poor man at his gate, atoned by bringing the stranger into his own room, and putting him in his bed. The commonest story in the lives of the saints, as in the life of St. Columban, is the one about a leper being taken in only to disappear suddenly, showing that it was Christ to whom hospitality had been shown. More than "angels unaware."

The official hospice, or guest house, appeared very early in Christian life. As early as the time of Constantine we find such houses of general hospitality, for the pilgrim, the traveler, the aged, the orphan, the needy of every description. It was chiefly the concern of the Bishop of the place who administered it through some of his clergy. But gradually the work had to be specialized. Hospitals, for instance, an outgrowth of the common hospice, came to be managed separately, for obvious reasons, and the hospice was given over solely to travelers. These hospices were run by hermits or monks. They gave free food and shelter. They increased in number rapidly since they were an absolute necessity, owing to the numerous pilgrimages to the Holy Land, to Rome and to other holy shrines, like the modern pilgrimages to Lourdes and Lisieux. The monks were called "the nurses of the poor," and every monastery was obliged to have a guest house. As Montalembert says, "they rendered honor to poverty." After Charlemagne the practical work for the poor was given over to the monks, and the monasteries became the center of activity, religious, cultural, charitable, and of all the other works of mercy. Not only did the monks give alms at the gate daily, but they tended the poor in their homes. But hospitality was their specialty. The Rule of St. Benedict was, "Let every stranger be received as if he were Christ Himself, for, it is Christ Himself who shall one day say to us, 'I was a stranger, and you took me in.'" And the Rule went on: "And let fitting honor be shown to all, especially such as are of the household of the faith, and to wayfarers. When, therefore, a guest is announced, let him be met by the superior or the brethren, with all due charity. Let them first pray together, and thus associate with one another in peace. At the arrival or departure of all guests, let Christ, who, indeed is received in their persons, be adored in them by bowing the head or even prostrating on the ground. Let the abbot pour water on the hands of the guests, and himself as well as the whole community wash their feet. Let special care be taken in the reception of the poor and of wayfarers, because in these Christ is more truly welcomed."

The most famous hospice in all the world was that founded, A.D. 962, by St. Bernard of Menthon in Switzerland. Everyone knows how through many centuries all the monks have risked their lives, and many have died, looking for the lost wayfarers. It is a perpetual parable of the Lost Sheep. They were heroes, not weaklings. Says Montalembert, "Monasteries were never intended to collect the invalids of the world." They worked, and all their substance they considered the patrimony of the poor. In one day, for instance, seventeen thousand people were helped. They always remembered the words of Bernard: "The friendship of the poor constitutes us the friends of Kings, but the love of poverty makes Kings of us." "We are the poor of Christ."

Most of the works of mercy, when practised on a big scale — as we have seen in the ransoming of captives — were required to meet a special need. This explains the phenomenal growth of the Military Orders in the Middle Ages. There have been at least a hundred. The Crusades gave rise to the chief ones, which provided a combination of military service and care of the sick and wayfarers. The most important one was that of the Order of the Hospital of St. John of Jerusalem, which later was known as the Knights of Rhodes, and finally as the Sovereign Order of the Knights of Malta. The Order existed before the Crusades but grew rapidly to provide for the needs of that period. It had humble beginnings. Some merchants of Amalfi had founded at Jerusalem in the eleventh century a convent, church, and hospital to look after the many pilgrims to the Holy Land. Charlemagne had founded a hospital there, but it had been destroyed by the Caliph. The gifts from the wealthy poured in so fast to the new establishment, that these "Brothers of the Hospitallers of St. John the Baptist" were enabled to found hospital after hospital. The society was composed of Knights, of noble birth, of priests, and of lay brothers, who took the three vows. It was a religious society, full of fervor and zeal, but the Knights continued to be Knights and fought against the Mussulmans, and eventually became the strong bulwark of the Christian power in the East. But side by side with the military activity went the humble work of the brother, nursing the sick and giving hospitality to pilgrims. There were also societies of women affiliated with the service.

Similar to the work of the Hospitallers of St. John
the Baptist was that of the Knights Templars in Jerusalem. They were never a big society, never exceeding
four hundred at one time, but they did wonderful work
of hospitality and kindred works of mercy. They declined
at last through the pride that came from their wealth
and power. There were dissensions, too, between the
Templars and the Hospitallers. When the Templars were
suppressed the Hospitallers (A.D. 1310) bought their
holdings, but at such a cost that it beggared them. Yet
as the Templars declined so also declined the Hospitallers, by departing from their original Rule. In 1310
they seized the Island of Rhodes. They existed thus for
two hundred years, but were finally conquered by the
Turks (1522), when they removed to the Island of Malta,
where they remained till 1798, when Napoleon seized the
Island. It would be a great mistake to think of these
Orders only in the terms of their decline. They had done
Christ's work for the strangers. They had met the need
when it existed. The Knights of Malta, for instance, had
delivered innumerable Christian slaves from the galleys.
All these orders — a hundred of them — had been harbors
for the harborless. Daily, for centuries, they had harbored
the Lord in the persons of His poor. The world is still
a better place because of these Knights of Christ.

The Crusading spirit of these orders increased everywhere the merciful work of harboring the harborless.
You will find it strong in the Franciscan, for example. St.
Francis had written in his Rule: "And whoever comes
to the brethren, friend or enemy, thief or robber, shall
be kindly received." The Franciscan ideal was, as Father
Cuthbert says, "an abandonment of oneself to faith in
the love of God for His creatures, and in the principle
of neighborly goodwill as the proper unitive element in
Christian society." And because of the law of Charity,
they made themselves, "servants to others, ministering to

others, both spiritually, and temporally out of that which in their poverty they had to give, namely the gift of human sympathy and service. Hence though they freely received of others, they also freely gave, taking as their example Jesus Christ in His earthly life."

Perhaps the loveliest manifestation of the work of mercy of harboring the harborless was the care of orphans. From the beginning God had taken over the cause of the father-less — "Who is the father of orphans, and the judge of widows" (Ps. 67:6). God's curse is many times pronounced upon those who neglect the orphans: "If you hurt them, they will cry out to me, and I will hear their cry; and my rage shall be enkindled, and I will strike you with the sword, and your wives shall be widows, and your children fatherless" (Exod. 22:22–24). Over and over the prophets Jeremias, Ezechiel, Zacharias, blast those who "have grieved the fatherless."

And our Lord put all the little ones under His special care: "Suffer the little children to come unto me and forbid them not. Of such is the Kingdom of Heaven."

To St. James (1:27) "religion pure and undefiled before God the Father is this: to give aid to orphans and widows in their tribulation, and to keep oneself unspotted from this world." Just there was the whole Christian Charter. To care for the orphan or the stranger hardly entered the pagan conception. The Romans had a slight conception of it; with the Greeks it was merely to raise citizens for the state, to which, like so many modern states, they believed the child solely belonged. They had no idea of producing citizens for the Kingdom of Heaven. There is a big difference. That item alone showed how infinitely superior Christianity is to paganism. Thus merciful hospitality was one of the first cares of the early Christians. Asylums for orphans were established very early. The Apostolic Constitutions had it, "Orphans as well as widows are always commended to Christian love." St. Augustine declared: "Your piety knows what care the Church and the bishops should take for the protection of all men but especially of orphan children." One of the offices of widows and deaconesses was to take orphans into their own homes. The first solicitude of the bishops and of the monasteries was for orphans. In our own day, when every diocese, every big city, has an orphanage we take it as a matter of course. We are apt to forget the pioneers who against tremendous odds fought the cause of the helpless little ones. Speak the name of St. Vincent de Paul, and at once you see him going through the streets of Paris at night collecting the abandoned infants. Say St. John Bosco, and at once you think of the reclaimed orphan boy. In truth you could fill page after page with just the names of holy men and women who devoted their lives to Christ's little ones. It is the same with all who harbor the harborless. The houses for the rescue of fallen women, as the Houses of the Good Shepherd; the homes of the Little Sisters of the Poor, who beg from door to door to keep a roof over the heads of unwanted old folks; homes and hospitals and asylums that care for every human ill — all these take literally the words of Christ: "I was a stranger and you took me in."

Personally we may never be called upon to share our home with a stranger. Yet we can share our heart with him. We can give to those who are doing the actual harboring. Helping them to do the work of mercy, we are making more confident the hope that when our little bark sets out on its last voyage and crosses the bar, our Divine Pilot will guide us into the safe Harbor of Eternal Love.

Mother of Mercy, bless this house where thy name is always blessed.

Chapter X

To Visit the Sick

IT IS this work of mercy that shows, if nothing else would show, the tremendous advance of the New Testament over the Old. You may search the Old Testament, and outside of the regulations for the treatment of leprosy — and they are numerous and very considerate — you will find few detailed mentions of the duty of kindness to the sick, as sick. It may be assumed that many of the commands as to the treatment of the "poor," the "needy," the "weak" included mercy to the sick. Still the impression remains that the people regarded sickness as the result of parental or personal sin. That idea is at the heart of the protests of the comforters of Job, that he must have sinned to have so many ills poured out upon him. The theme of the Book of Job, however, is that sickness and material want were God's trial of his patience, and not a direct punishment for sin. Even in the time of our Lord the popular conception was that sickness was a punishment for sin. When He cured the man who had been blind from birth, His disciples asked Him: "Rabbi, who has sinned, this man or his parents, that he should be born blind?"

Jesus answered: "Neither has this man sinned, nor his parents: but the works of God were to be made manifest in him" (John 9:2–3).

It was rather a hopeless background, and for that reason our Lord's miraculous healing of the sick, with no questions asked, shines forth with Divine light. If one were asked to confine his description of the work of Jesus to one statement, he would at once think of His kindness to the sick, and express His mission in these words: "He went about doing good." True, the miraculous cures worked by Him had the fundamental object of proving the Divinity of His mission. When He was asked by the committee sent by John the Baptist if He were the Messias, He pointed to His works. "Go and report to John what you have heard and seen: the blind see, the lame walk, the lepers are cleansed, the deaf hear . . . the poor have the gospel preached to them" (Matt. 11:4–5). But not alone was His care of man's ills a "sign"; it was the infinite pity flooding from His Sacred Heart; and we can well surmise that many a cure of the sick, sometimes unrecorded, was not done primarily to sanction His Gospel, but in tender compassion just for an individual soul. He began His mission with that sympathy: "Blessed are the merciful, for they shall obtain mercy." "Blessed are they who mourn, for they shall be comforted." "And Jesus was going about all Galilee teaching in their synagogues, and preaching the gospel of the kingdom, and healing every disease and every sickness among the people . . . and they brought to him all the sick suffering from various diseases and torments, those possessed, and lunatics and paralytics; and he cured them" (Matt. 4:23–24). That test is all inclusive, and is repeated over and over in similar words. "And wherever they went . . . they laid the sick in the market-places, and entreated him to let them touch but the tassel of his cloak; and as many as touched him were saved" (Mark 6: 56). It was ever the same story: "Many followed him, and he cured them all."

St. Matthew sees in it the fulfillment of the words of Isaias: "Surely he hath borne our infirmities and carried our sorrows: and we have thought him as it were a leper and as one struck by God and afflicted" (53:4). The cure of the leper, the paralytic at Capharnaum, Peter's mother-in-law, the man with the withered hand, the daughter of Jairus, the woman with a hemorrhage, the daughter of the Canaanite woman, the deaf man, the blind man, the possessed boy, the blind Bartimaeus, the Centurion's servant, the demoniac, the two blind men, the blind men at Jericho; the raising of the son of the widow of Naim, the raising of Lazarus — What a great place these and other cures take up in the Gospels!

And not only did He Himself exercise these healing powers, but He gave the power of exercising them to His disciples: "Cure the sick, raise the dead, cleanse the lepers, cast out devils" (Matt. 10:8). "And they cast out many devils, and anointed with oil many sick people, and healed them" (Mark 6:13).

The essence of His teaching in regard to the sick is contained in His parable of the Good Samaritan — that kindness should be shown by all to all — since He set up as the example of mercy the kindness done by a despised Samaritan, when even the priest and Levite had failed.

One must be struck by the prevalence of sickness in our Lord's time. To a great extent it is the same today in Palestine. But before Christianity was preached the condition of the sick there was deplorable. Little attention was paid to them. Sickness was regarded as an unavoidable evil, and death under distressing conditions was common. The doctors were no good. Anatomy was forbidden to the Jews, hence little was known about the science of medicine. In the matter of blindness, so common then, and very common today, due much to the fine dust and the glaring sun on the white ground, it helps us to understand why there are so many exultant references to the cure of these unfortunates.

When our Lord finished His work of healing on this earth and returned to His Father, He left that power to heal as a mark of the authority of His apostles.

The *Acts* relate many cures. "They carried the sick into the streets and laid them on beds and pallets, that, when Peter passed, his shadow at least might fall on some of them. And there came also multitudes from the towns near Jerusalem, bringing the sick and those troubled with unclean spirits, and they were all cured" (5:15–16). The cure of the lame beggar, of Aeneas the paralytic, the raising of Tabitha, the cure of the lame man at Lystra, of the young man at Troas, of the father of Publius at Malta — all are instances of the important part played by healing in the establishment of the Church. The people knew the power of the Apostles. "Handkerchiefs and aprons were carried from his [Paul's] body to the sick" (19:12).

The cure of the sick was not only used as a proof of the Gospel; it was even made the effect of a sacrament, Extreme Unction, and this alone shows how new a part the sick man was to play in the exercise of works of mercy. "Is any one among you sick? Let him bring in the presbyters of the Church, and let them pray over him, anointing him with oil in the name of the Lord. And the prayer of faith shall save the sick man, and the Lord shall raise him up; and if he be in sins, they shall be forgiven him" (James 5:14–15).

The example of the Divine Physician has been paramount in the Church. It would be impossible to estimate the miraculous cures, from the days of the Apostles to Lourdes.

But the Church has busied herself not so much with working miracles as with tending the person of Christ in the person of the sick. She has never forgotten the word to be spoken at the great assize: "I was sick and you visited me."

That love for the sick is peculiar to Christianity. Paganism never guessed it. As Dean Farrar says: "Amid all the boasted civilization of antiquity there existed no hospitals, no penitentiaries; no asylums." That is not abso-

lutely true. Even some of the pagan temples, as in Egypt
and Greece, had medical clinics attached to them, and the
sick were brought to the temples. In Ireland, even three
hundred years before Christ, there were hospitals, called
"Houses of Sorrow." But this was so only with the civilized
pagans, for the savage tribes often put to death the useless
sick. All the pagans considered sickness a curse of the
gods, and any care they gave the sick was more of a
propitiation of the offended powers. Again, it was chiefly
a move for civic betterment, and did not have any real
religious motive; certainly it was not for the love of God,
or even real love of neighbor. No religion, no real hospital. As St. Augustine says, "Hospitals have their origin
in the truth of religion."

The first real hospital mentioned is the one founded
by the Roman matron, Fabiola, at Rome. St. Jerome calls
it "the first of all," and he knew. Fabiola was a rich noble
lady who was married to a profligate. She finally divorced
him and married another. She was struck with remorse,
and as one means of doing penance, she used her great
wealth in turning her country house into a refuge for the
sick poor, who up to that time had no one to care for
them, but lay stretched in the streets. She tended them
herself.

It is not strange that the hospital idea grew so rapidly.
After all, Christian charity, as we see from the Epistles,
was well organized from the beginning. A regular institution was impossible during the persecutions; but as soon
as the Church came from the catacombs there was an open
effort to meet every need, material as well as spiritual.
There was need of such charity, for after Constantine, the
general state of the people, due to economic conditions,
was deplorable, especially among the poor.

Bishops like St. Basil and St. Gregory Nazianzen tended
the sick with their own hands, and were helped by men
and women of the highest rank. The hospital erected by

St. Basil was as big as a town. St. John Chrysostom spent all he could get on building new hospitals and repairing old ones.

Soon the hospital became a necessary institution in every diocese all over the Christian world. Charlemagne, for instance, ordered that a hospital be attached to every cathedral and monastery. The bishops and priests were in the beginning the mainstay of the hospitals, but as the monastic institutions grew, as well as the Military Orders, the work of specializing devolved more and more on the monks.

Every monastery had an infirmary attached to it for its own members, and naturally this became the model for every hospital. Most of them stemmed from the Benedictines. The vow made by the monks is beautiful. "I make a vow of poverty, charity and hospitality, and I bind myself to serve the poor on their recovery, though they shall be infidels, and suffering from contagious diseases."

Every ill was provided for, even insanity. In fact, in the Middle Ages the work of caring for the sick was a big business. Hospitals were as numerous as they are today. It would be impossible to catalogue the many orders, societies, confraternities, guilds, which had as their first aim the care of the sick. They were far more numerous in the Middle Ages than they are today. We have never quite repaired the damage done by the Reformation. The destruction of the monasteries, the closing of the hospitals, the confiscation of endowments and other property that really did not belong to the monks but to the poor was not only the destruction of property but the destruction of an ideal. Even Luther had to complain that his followers neglected the sick and the poor. It was what St. Augustine had said: "If any one fall from faith, necessarily he must fall from Charity." That, in one word, expresses the Reformation.

The Council of Trent tried to repair the damage. It

insisted again that the bishops provide for the poor, and especially supervise the hospitals and their funds. The need was exposed, and, as usual in the Church, there was response to the need. New orders arose; over one hundred orders of women alone. The chief response, of course, came from St. Vincent de Paul.

But it always had been a Catholic tradition to take care of the sick. It had been a peculiarly Franciscan ideal. Francis used to say to his friars, "In the sick you see the infirmities which He took upon Himself for our sakes." Once when he was sick he noticed that the friar who had the care of him seemed impatient. So he called him to his bed and said, "And when you are weary of me, keep always before your eyes that the Lord will reward you for all that you do for me." Hence he made it a rule for the Third Order that the sick were to be visited once a week, to be helped corporally, as well as to be admonished spiritually. His Rule had it: "Blessed is the servant of God who loves his brother as much when the brother is sick and depends on him, as when the brother is well and can be of use and pleasure to him." The service of the sick entered largely into the early life of the Franciscan friars and nuns. The story is told that once Francis and Brother Bernard started on a pilgrimage to Compostella. They came across a sick man. Francis ordered Bernard to stay behind and take care of him. So Bernard missed the pilgrimage. But he did not complain. The sick — or Christ — came first.

But the Christlike kindness of Francis was seen in his care of lepers. He always spoke of them as "My brother Christians." He loved them. We recall that his real conversion came, when, much against his grain, he embraced a leper, to find that it was Jesus Christ. So he made the care of lepers the first test of candidates for his order. For a long time the Franciscans settled near the leper houses. All through the Middle Ages the leper was viewed

as an image of Jesus Christ, and countless are the stories
of the assisted leper turning out to be Jesus Christ Himself. So, too, we have the old story of St. Martin kissing
the leper and curing with the kiss. Hence the lepers became the object of special care, and even a special order,
The Knights of St. Lazarus, was founded for the purpose.
In the thirteenth century there is reported to have been
nineteen thousand leper houses in Europe, two thousand
of them in France alone. There was a leper house at
Assisi, and Francis, after his sudden conversion, went there
to tend the lepers, even kissing their hands. Later on he
lived at the leper house at Gubbio, where he would wash
the feet of the lepers, treat their sores, and even kiss them.
To him they were "my brother lepers," as they were to
Father Damien, who surpassed everyone else in devotion
to these unfortunate beings.

Often Francis would send a stray leper to St. Clare,
who would care for him, sometimes cure him, seeing Jesus
Christ in him. She personally took care of the sick sisters
in her convent: "As she was wont she took with her some
good medicines which she knew how to use." She would
make the Sign of the Cross over them and even heal them.
When the sisters came home at night, she washed their
feet. Many a night she would get up to cover the sisters,
lest they might get a chill.

The idea was followed by St. Elizabeth of Hungary.
She would bring the sick poor from their hovels and lodge
them in the castle. She fitted up a hospital there, and personally cared for the sick every day. "How well it is with
us," she said, "that we are allowed to bathe and cover
our Lord." She also founded three confraternities for the
care of the sick.

There never was a better friend to the sick than St.
Catherine of Siena. The great hospital of *Santa Maria della
Scala* — Siena had other hospitals — founded by the Re-
public and containing an infirmary, a foundling asylum,

and a guest house of pilgrims, and all run by a voluntary brotherhood, was surpassed in many ways by no modern hospital. It still functions. The Rule read that the brethren should wait upon the sick and feed them: "and each brother shall carry upon him a knife without a point wherewith to cut bread and other food for the sick." But the chief aid was to be spiritual: "Likewise the nurses attending to the sick and the servants must have a care to tell the sick to confess their sins and receive the sacraments of the Church." So that the care of the sick was an old Sienese custom, and very early Catherine learned the art. She was but a year old when the Great Plague, or Black Death, swept over Europe (1348) when nearly four million died, with consequences from which the world still suffers. It was horrible. It came back to Siena in 1374. The streets were filled with corpses. Catherine had always been an attendant at the hospitals, working night and day. Her specialty was to care for such trying patients as no one else wanted. Often she got no thanks, but only abuse and calumny. Twice a day she went to the Lazaretto. She tamed everybody, even the most hardened sinners. Thus when the plague came she was a seasoned veteran. With her smelling salts and lantern she toiled ceaselessly. Six of her little nieces and nephews died. She buried them with her own hands.

That spirit of love for the sick never ceased in the Church. It had a special flowering in the work of St. Vincent de Paul and his Daughters of Charity. The work done by him in every branch of mercy seems incredible. His work in founding the Sisters through Louise de Marillac was a Divine inspiration. One dreads to think of what would have happened to the world if the Sisters of Charity had not come along. They had an obscure beginning, just simple peasant girls, humble helpers in the hospitals, not even trained nurses. But soon they were the dominant factor, thanks to St. Vincent and Louise. It was the Spirit

of God in them. As St. Vincent put it in their Rule: "The
Sister infirmarian who has the care of the sick should
work in union with, and after the example of Him who
was full of compassion for all who were in suffering, and
who healed them of their diseases." And Louise wrote of
the invalid sisters: "I beg of our Saviour to give you the
grace of His own spirit, so that you should support and
assist them in the spirit of Charity and sweetness for the
sake of His holy love." Not only the Sisters, but great
ladies, princesses even, were persuaded by Vincent to devote themselves to the hospitals. Once a visitor to the
hospital of Bruges said: "I could almost say that my idea
of Heaven is a place filled with Sisters of Charity." The
sixteenth century, though a time of great religious up-
heaval, shines out as an era of mercy to the sick.

St. Teresa, busy foundress as she was, always made time
for the sick, bringing them whatever dainties she could
afford. "Thank God," she would say, whenever she received gifts of fruit, "for giving me something for my dear
sick people." She would hide the oranges and lemons in
her sleeve and take them to the patients, and come back
beaming because she had been able to make them happy.
"I also commend the sick nuns to your care," she wrote
to Ven. Anne of Jesus; "treat them very kindly, for, believe
me, the day you leave the sick in want, you will be in
want of everything yourself." She made many regulations
for the care of the sick, as of prime importance. "If you
see a sick sister whom you can relieve, never fear losing
your devotion; compassionate her, if she is in pain, feel
for it as if it were your own, and when there is need, fast
so that she may eat, not so much for her sake as because
you know Our Lord asks it of you."

When you think of the sick, necessarily you see the
picture of St. Camillus de Lellis, the converted gambler
and tramp, who, after a long novitiate of serving the sick,
established his order of "The Fathers of a Good Death,"

vowed to care for the plague stricken, in hospitals and private homes. An invalid himself for forty-six years, he would crawl on his hands and knees to care for the sick.

The work of visiting the sick has a special appeal to all of us. There are some works of mercy which we may not be in a position to perform. But always we can be kind to the sick. We can visit them, bring them a sympathetic word if we can bring nothing else. We can pray for them, seeking the healing of their soul as well as the solace of their pains. There are more prayers in the Ritual for the Visiting of the Sick than for any other occasion. Sometimes occasion demands that we see that the sick person receives the Sacraments, especially the Great Sacrament for the sick, Extreme Unction. Our Lady is proclaimed in an old Greek hymn:

> Hail! healing of my Body!
> Hail! safety of my soul!

We should continually commit our sick to the care of her who learned the art of consoling at the sickbed of St. Joseph, but, more, at the deathbed of her own merciful Son.

Mother of Mercy, Health of the Sick, pray for us!

Chapter XI

To Bury the Dead

TO PAY the last honors to the dead bodies of our loved ones is one of our tenderest obligations. Sacrifices are endured willingly, burdens are taken on so that the departed may have becoming, or decent, burial. The danger is not in doing too little, but in vanity, in overexaggerating the importance of the trappings of mourning.

This respect for the dead body of a loved one is deeply embedded in our nature. No matter how far back you go in history, you cannot find a people, even barbarous, that did not concern itself with some kind of funeral rites. Relationship had no more solemn duty than to provide the last honors over the final resting place. To deny those last honors to a man was the greatest disgrace that could be shown his memory and the reputation of his survivors. We recall how beautifully the theme is treated in the *Antigone* of Sophocles. The two brothers of Antigone had been slain. One of them, Eteocles, had been burned; the other, Polynices, at the order of the King, had been denied burial.

> Unwept, unsepulchred, a dainty prize
> For fowl that watch gloating upon their prey

Antigone performed the burial rites for him, and was put to death for the act of love to her brother. Burial with the pagans had a religious significance. The Greeks had great respect for the dead. The law was, "If a man fail to adorn the sepulchre of his dead parents, the magistrates must take note of it and enquire."

The funeral procession is the oldest of all, and we find recorded in the earliest ages the carrying of lighted torches as part of the ceremonial of burial. But the Egyptians, of all ancient peoples, had, perhaps, the greatest concern for the dead. They were not content with mere burial, but had invented all the arts of embalming, or mummifying the body. It was the effort to put away corruption indefinitely and to obtain a material immortality. No doubt in their burial customs there was a lot of superstition, but as there was always a prayer that the departed soul might revisit the body — hence the supplies of food, utensils, buried in the tomb — there would seem to be some glimmer of a belief in the resurrection of the body. The very act of burial indicated the urge to survival. For with this exception of the Egyptians, the general custom with the pagans, as with the Greeks and Romans, was to burn, or cremate, the body; although the Greeks and Romans sometimes buried, sometimes cremated, according to their idea as to an afterlife. Cremation, then as now, indicated a denial of the resurrection of the body. Cremation was never practised by the Egyptians, and never by the Jews except when there was danger of pestilence, as in time of war.

The Jews always buried their dead, and usually in sepulchers. You will find the custom referred to many times in the Old Testament. To be buried in the land of Israel was popularly believed to aid in winning God's mercy. There was further the natural wish of the Jews to lie with their own people. "Bury me," said Jacob, "with my fathers in the double cave" (Gen. 49: 29). Joseph obeyed this behest and had Jacob embalmed according to the Jewish custom. Thus he brought his father back home, while "there went with him all the ancients of Pharaoh's house and all the elders of the land of Egypt." Joseph ordered his brethren that when he died they would carry his bones out of Egypt, "out of this place."

At the time of the Exodus Moses brought Joseph's bones with him, and the Israelites kept them through all the years of wandering, and finally buried them in Sichem, in the field of Jacob. So, too, we find King David sending messengers to the men of Jabes Galaad, to say, "Blessed be you to the Lord, who have shown this mercy to your master Saul, and have buried him" (2 Kings 2:5). It was an accursed thing to be deprived of burial among one's own people. So the old prophet said to the disobedient prophet (3 Kings 13:22): "Thy dead body shall not be brought into the sepulchre of thy fathers." When the Jews were in captivity, one of the punishments inflicted upon them by the conquerors was that they were forbidden to bury their dead. It is related in the Book of Tobias that one day an Israelite was killed in the street. Tobias left his dinner, went out, took the body, hid it and at sunset buried it. Later on when he was blinded, he was reproached by his friends: "where is thy hope, for which thou gavest alms and didst bury the dead?" (2:4–16.) So the worst Jeremias could say of Joakim was: "He shall be buried with the burial of an ass, rotten and cast forth without the gates of Jerusalem" (Jer. 22:19).

At the time of our Lord, and very likely it was an immemorial tradition, the burial etiquette was very strict. A man who touched a corpse was defiled, nevertheless great respect was paid to the corpse. At the burial there were weepers and flutists and every demonstration of mourning. After the return of the funeral procession from the tomb, the mourners would sit on the ground, their feet bare, their heads veiled, while, during seven days of solemn mourning, they received the condolences of their friends.

Our Lord, while referring to His own death and burial, did not seem to insist on any duty to the dead. When one of His disciples said to Him, "Lord, let me first go and bury my father," He replied, "Leave the dead to bury their own dead, but do thou go and proclaim the kingdom of God" (Luke 9:60–61). It was the soul that was important. "And do not be afraid of those who kill the body but cannot kill the soul. But rather be afraid of him who is able to destroy both soul and body in hell" (Matt. 10:28). Our Lord's insistence was on the spiritual. It was not that He wished to destroy the Jewish custom as to fitting burial or to release men from their obligation to show respect to the dead. When John the Baptist was killed, his disciples came and took away his body and buried it. Jesus prophesied as to His own anointing and burial, and when He was dead Joseph of Arimathea begged His body of Pilate, "And he took him down, and wrapped him in a linen cloth, and laid him in a rock-hewn tomb where no one had ever yet been laid" (Luke 23:53).

Thus it was in accordance with the long traditions of the Jews, and in memory of the burial of the Lord, that the first Christians buried their dead, and surrounded the burial and the tomb with all possible reverence. When Stephen was stoned to death, "devout men took care of Stephen's burial and made great lamentation over him" (Acts 8:2–3).

It was natural that the Christians should make much of the dead body. The dead Christ had risen from the grave, and, after Him, as "the first fruits of them that sleep" (1 Cor. 15:20), every man would rise from the dead on the last day. The Christian should imitate Christ, even to burial. So from the beginning Christian burial was accompanied by a religious ceremony. The Church did not eliminate the customary pomp, but sanctified it while protesting against too much pomp. The Christians never had any thought of cremating the dead. That was an en-

tirely pagan custom, with false religious beliefs as the
background; hence it could never be tolerated. It was too
much bound up with fire worship, with rank materialism.
The pagans, indeed, often burned the bodies of the martyrs as a protest against the Christian teaching of the
resurrection of the body. And that is why the Church
today continues to condemn cremation. In itself it makes
little difference whether a body is reduced to ashes at
once by fire or by the slow process of disintegration in the
earth, and under certain conditions the Church does permit it. However, because of its anti-Christian character
and purpose the general law of the Church forbids it.
It may be noted that the Freemasons were the first to obtain permission for it from various governments. The
Church has always respected the body as having been the
temple of the Holy Ghost, and destined to be glorified.
It had shared in the life of grace and virtue, a member of
Jesus Christ. If a Catholic orders that his body be cremated, he cannot be given Christian burial. The Church
tolerates no semblance of disrespect to the dead body. We
find, for instance, Pope Boniface VIII (A.D. 1300) making
it a cause for excommunication *ipso facto* to disembowel
bodies in order to facilitate their transportation to be
buried in other lands. So sacred was the body of the
Christian that it was buried apart from the pagans. The
ground was consecrated where the Christian lay waiting
for the resurrection. And in Christian law it is a crime
to violate a grave.

The Church has always looked upon her cemetery as a
sacred place. The word itself, meaning place of rest, was
applied to a tomb or a general graveyard, and was dis-
tinctive of Jews or Christians, never used by pagans. It
was the term at first applied to the catacombs. At first
Christians were buried with Jews, but that custom soon
ceased, because, for one reason, the Jews considered the
dead body unclean. Thus the Roman catacombs soon be-

came entirely Christian. They were the first churchyard, indeed the first churches, where the Christian mysteries were performed amid the tombs of the faithful. We are apt to regard the catacombs as secret places, but there could have been no secrecy about such tremendous places, fifty catacombs, five hundred miles of galleries, with two million graves; the only secrecy was about the Christian mysteries celebrated there. Burial, even in those days, had to be a big business, and the Christians had their own burial societies, which they supported. Even the matter of digging graves was a big business. The grave diggers were not esteemed in pagan society, but with the Christians it was a holy job, and they ranked with the inferior clergy and were paid from the common treasury. It was a life of great sacrifice. Highly honored, too, were the artists who decorated the tombs.

Much of the Christian activity was centered in the catacombs. The *Agape,* or "love feast," preceding the Eucharistic Supper, later became merely a funeral memorial.

The regard which the Church had for the proper burial of the dead may be gathered from the Fathers. We learn that the first Christians kept their dead exposed for three days, clothed in as precious habits as possible. They were watched over in prayer — our modern wake — and then they were carried to the tomb, with lighted tapers, and to the music of hymns, expressing belief in the resurrection of the body. St. Jerome says it was customary to sing *Alleluia!* The body was buried with its insignia of rank, or, in the case of martyrs, with the instrument of torture, or phials of blood, and also with the Acts of their martyrdom, crosses, or copies of the Gospel. At the time of St. Augustine corpses were not allowed to be buried within the city walls. St. Augustine wrote a book, "On the Care of the Dead," in answer to St. Paulinus, once a Roman Senator, and then porter of the Church of St. Felix Nola, where many wished to be buried. He wrote: "All these things, the care of a funeral, the kind of sepulture, the pomp of obsequies, are rather comforts for the living than helps for the dead." But he also said: "The bodies of the faithful are not to be despised and cast out, since they were the organs and vessels used by the Holy Spirit. Dear and venerable is a paternal vest or ring, and in like manner should we honor the body which was more joined and familiar to us than any garment which we wear, which served not as an external ornament or assistance, but which belonged to the very nature of man. Our Lord commended the woman who had prepared ointments for his burial; and in the Gospel he is commemorated with praise who diligently and reverently gave Him sepulture."

St. Augustine had common sense about burial. When, at the sack of Rome, the Christians were taunted that the bodies of the slain could not be buried, Augustine practically replied, "What's the difference?" "It was neither fault in the living who could not perform the rights, nor hurt to the dead that could not feel them." And he quotes the pagan poet:

Who wants a grave, Heaven serveth for a tomb.

All things being equal, it is the ordinary Christian duty to provide a decent burial. It is always noted as a work of religion, a work of mercy. The bodies of the martyrs were the object of special care. When, for example, St. Sebastian was killed, his body was thrown into a sewer, but a Roman lady recovered it and buried it in the catacombs. We are told that St. Marcellinus, Pope, deemed himself unworthy of Christian burial, so he remained unburied for thirty-five days. St. Peter appeared to his successor, St. Marcellus, and asked why he, Peter, was kept so long without burial. He said: "As long as I shall see Marcellinus deprived of burial, I shall consider myself unburied."

So important was burial considered, that it is common

enough to read in the lives of the saints that they were buried miraculously when there was no one to do service to them. So a lion dug the grave of St. Mary of Egypt, and two lions dug the grave of St. Paul the Hermit.

In the Middle Ages there was an especially tender love for the dead and care of the remains. So the Guilds, besides being interested in every work of mercy and in the betterment of the condition of the workingman were to a great extent burial societies. Their constitutions guaranteed a certain number of Masses to the dead members. There were special organizations to bury the dead, especially the poor. The chief one was the *"Misericordia,"* founded by a Sienese nobleman in Florence, in 1244, and still in existence. It embraced every rank of society. The members helped also in hospital work. In their burial work they wore a black hood and crucifix, and with lighted candles came at evening to carry the dead to the Misericordia Cemetery.

One of the rules of the Third Order of St. Francis was to pray for the deceased members and to attend the burials. It was told of Brother Giles that he carried bodies to the grave to support himself. The most distinguished citizens sought to arrange to have themselves and families buried in Franciscan churches.

St. Elizabeth of Hungary would wrap the dead in sheets from her own bed, and would follow her poorest subjects to the grave.

The story is told of a poor Dominican brother that when he was dying St. Mark came to him, and said of him: "Because he was close to me, and often visited the place where my body rests, for this reason I have come to aid him in this hour." That is one of the tenderest things about the saints, their association with the dead, not in any silly spiritualistic sense, but in the common sense of the Communion of saints. To them no one is absolutely dead. They are like the little girl in Words-

worth's poem, "We Are Seven." Asked how many sisters
and brothers she had, she replied:

> Seven are we;
> And two of us at Conway dwell,
> And two are gone to sea.
> Two of us in the church-yard lie,
> My sister and my brother;
> And, in the church-yard cottage, I
> Dwell near them with my mother.

"But they are dead; these two are dead!" protested the
poet. But the child still replied, "We are seven!" She had
their little graves to prove it. Are not the cemetery paths
the road to heaven? What a lovely name for the cemetery:
"God's Acre!" There the bodies are sown in corruption,
to rise one day in incorruption. That is why the Church
makes so much of Christian burial, and urges her children to visit the cemeteries. It is for the primary purpose,
of course, of getting prayers for the souls, but also to do
honor to the dust of the dead. All who visit a cemetery
during the octave of All Souls and pray there for the
dead, even mentally only, may gain a Plenary Indulgence
under the usual conditions, on each day of the octave —
the indulgence being applicable only to the dead. So also
those who on any day of the year make such a visit, praying for the Holy Souls, may gain for them a partial Indulgence of seven years. It is a combination of the corporal and spiritual works of mercy, to be kind to the body
and soul of the dead. How the Church regards the cemetery is seen in the prayers and ceremonies of the Pontifical
Blessing for a cemetery. It is a long ritual, one of the
longest, with the blessing of the five crosses, the prayers,
and even a Preface, which is found only in the very
solemn rites. The theme of all the prayers is to beg God
to bless the cemetery, "that the human bodies resting
here, after the course of life, may on the great day of
Judgment together with the happy souls, merit to obtain

the joys of everlasting life, through Jesus Christ Our Lord."

There is hardly any need to urge our Catholic people to attend the burial of the dead, or to show respect to their remains, and to their last resting place. There is rather more danger of too much material display and of extravagant funerals. Natural sympathy and grief urge a man to loving care of the dead, but the care should be spiritualized. We should assist at the burial of our dead as if we were assisting at the entombment of Christ. "Inasmuch as ye have done it to me." In that way we make it a true corporal work of mercy, and store up treasures against the day of our own burial when we will need so much the rewarding mercy of Christ, "Come ye blessed."

Mother of Mercy, who helped to bury Jesus,
Queen of Pity, pray for us at the hour of death!

THE SPIRITUAL WORKS OF MERCY

Chapter XII

To Admonish the Sinner

JUST as the life is more than the meat, the soul more than the body, so the alms that immediately concern the salvation of the soul are more important than those that concern the body. So the spiritual works of mercy are higher than the corporal, though, as St. Francis de Sales says, the common run of people prefer temporal alms-giving to spiritual — bodily mortification to the mortification of the heart.

And just as all the corporal works of mercy may be grouped under the heading of corporal alms, so all the spiritual works of mercy may be grouped under fraternal correction, or admonishing of the sinner, which is, indeed, spiritual alms. So it is that fraternal correction is the only one of the spiritual works of mercy that is ordinarily treated of specifically in theology.

In the Scriptures, both in the Old and the New Testament, fraternal correction is regarded as of prime importance. Even as early as Leviticus (19:17) the law is given: "Thou shalt not hate thy brother in thy heart, but reprove him openly, lest thou incur sin through him."

The Lord condemned Heli, the High Priest, "because

he knew that his sons did wickedly, and did not chastize them" (1 Kings 3:13). "Rebuke a wise man and he will love thee," says Proverbs (9:8). Proverbs repeats over and over the wisdom of accepting reproof and the folly of rejecting it. Ecclesiasticus, too, has many things to say on the theme "How good is it, when thou art reproved, to show repentance!" (20:4.)

The Prophets, whose whole life was devoted to reproving others for the purpose of amending them, mince no words about fraternal correction. If you do not correct your neighbor when it is necessary, God will impute His blood to you. Isaias prophesied of the Messiah that He would "reprove with equity." I regret being unable to quote all the Old Testament texts, for they build up a formidable argument in favor of fraternal correction.

But the duty is made even plainer in the New Testament. Our Lord did not hesitate to exercise correction. Time and again He proclaimed His woe! woe!

He was ever reproving the Scribes and Pharisees as whited sepulchers. Not content with reproving evil, He laid down the law by which His followers would exercise fraternal correction. "But if thy brother sin against thee, go and show him his fault, between thee and him alone. If he listen to thee, thou hast won thy brother. But if he do not listen to thee, take with thee one or two more, so that on the word of two or three witnesses every word may be confirmed. And if he refuse to hear them, appeal to the Church, but if he refuse to hear even the Church, let him be to thee as the heathen and the publican" (Matt. 18:15–18).

St. Paul adds his development of this instruction: "Do not rebuke an elderly man, but exhort him as you would a father, and young men as brothers, elderly women as mothers, younger women as sisters in all chastity" (1 Tim. 5:1–2). Again: "A factious man avoid after a first and a second admonition" (Titus 3:10–11). "Brethren, even if a person is caught doing something wrong, you who are spiritual instruct such a one in a spirit of meekness, considering thyself lest thou also be tempted" (Gal. 6:1).

And finally St. James has it: "He who causes a sinner to be brought back from his misguided way, will save his soul from death, and will cover a multitude of sins" (5:20).

It is on these texts that the moral theology of fraternal correction has been established.

Now, in correction we must be careful to make distinctions: There is first of all a judicial correction which has reference to justice. It is a vindictive, or punishing, correction, exercised publicly and for the common good by legitimate superiors, both to punish the offense and to protect the public. That is not our concern here. Fraternal correction, on the other hand, is more concerned with charity. It is the attempt to correct one's neighbor for his own good, to help him to save his soul. In a word, it is a spiritual alms, or act of mercy, to him. It is a private correction of our neighbor, with little reference to the public. It is the effort to recall him from sin to virtue, or to prevent him from falling into sin; or, as St. Thomas has it, a brotherly admonition to a sinner to persuade him to mend his ways. There is no thought of vengeance, of getting even, of humiliating a man — that end might easily lead to detraction — but simply, out of love for him, to help him spiritually. This may be done in many ways: by exhorting him, by teaching him, by appealing to his better nature, and so on.

Now, this is not to be considered as a mere whim on our part, as a holier-than-thou interest. It is commanded us by Divine Revelation, as seen above, and is incumbent upon us by natural and positive law, for the reason that as we are bound to prevent our neighbor's loss of life, so much the more are we bound to prevent his loss of soul. St. Augustine declares that it is an act of charity, and we must not deprive our neighbor of it, since, if he were to die in mortal sin through our failure to correct or warn him, we should be responsible for his loss.

A serious obligation presumes, of course, a corresponding serious matter. Hence, to make the correction binding under pain of mortal sin, the correction must concern a mortal sin, either committed or in serious danger of being committed. It is plain that if it be a question of venial sin only, the obligation to correct is only venial. To bind a man seriously, then, to fraternal correction, certain conditions are required. First he must know for sure that a serious sin has been committed or is about to be committed; second, there must be a hope that the admonition will be heeded; third, the person who does the correcting must be the proper one to do so, and he must feel assured that his efforts will do no grave harm to himself, and that by making it he is not rendering more hopeless the spiritual condition of the person he is trying to reform; and finally he must be convinced that there is need for him to do the correcting.

All then are bound to give correction when and where it is needed. The thought to make central is the spiritual welfare of our neighbor — who is drowning and needs our help.

Some have a special obligation. Superiors are more strictly bound to correct their subjects. Parents are bound to correct their children. So, too, the preacher is greatly responsible for the salvation of his hearers. The higher the position, the greater the obligation. All these are specific obligations. But no one is exempt. Fraternal correction may be given to an equal, even to a superior. Witness the examples of St. Catherine of Siena and St. Bridget of Sweden.

But — and it is an important point — even when all this is said, it may be stated generally that the ordinary person is usually excused from a serious obligation to correct his neighbor. This is due to many reasons. He may be unsuited for the task, indeed he may be the last one that should attempt it; again, it may be a thankless job, if there is no hope for the conversion of the one at fault; again, the corrector may have little opportunity to correct properly; and finally, there may be great danger, a tremendous inconvenience to him, if he tries to correct that certain party. After all, a man cannot go around correcting everybody. Such a man is a pest, a busybody, and generally does more harm than good. Hence, since the necessary conditions are not present, the grave obligation is rare for private individuals, save when there is immediate danger to the spiritual welfare of the neighbor. Even then we should bear in mind the sage counsel of St. Thomas when he says: "Acts of virtue must not be done anyhow (i.e., in any old way), but by observing the due circumstances which are requisite in order that an act may be virtuous; namely, that it be done, when, where, and how it might be done." Finally, we shall ask God to give His grace to the admonition.

St. Augustine warns us not to be spies, or snoopers, but to correct only what we see. In a person's zeal to correct, there often is danger of rash judgment. Ordinarily it is a good plan to mind our own business, get the beam out of our own eye, and sit back and pray. The great spiritual director, Abbé Huvelin, used to say, "Mistrust your zeal for doing good to others."

Our Lord once said to St. Catherine of Siena: "Reprove in general, and not in particular, unless thou shouldst have had an express revelation from Me; in that case thou shouldst with humility blame thyself and thy neighbor at the same time." But if one is really convinced that in a certain case he is obliged to correct his neighbor, then there is a sure method for him to follow. He should have the purest motive of charity, not one arising from a personal grudge. In dealing with an erring neighbor, he should be fatherly — a drop of honey catches more flies than a barrel of

vinegar; if he is dealing with an equal he should be mild
and loving; and if perchance with a superior, then in all
reverence and humility. In a word, fraternal correction
is an act of love, and should be done lovingly. It is an
alms, an act of mercy.

Outstanding in the lives of the saints is the conviction
of the obligation to aid one's neighbor by correction.
They hated sin, but they loved the sinner. To reclaim
him they stopped at nothing. They had no qualms about
fine points of etiquette; they deemed a man's salvation
more important than a recognition of the social amenities.
Bossuet speaks of the "outspokenness of the saints." They
were prophets of the Lord and they minced no words.
Sabatier says that the medieval saints occupied much the
same position in relation to the ecclesiastical system as
the prophets to the Jewish priesthood. They did not hesitate to denounce iniquity in the high places. Since, however, they were often inspired, it does not mean that the
ordinary man should imitate them.

But even when the correction given by the saints was
severe, it was given in all charity. The prayer of St. Augustine before writing against any adversary was, "Lord, put
kindness in my heart, that in fighting for the love of truth
I may not lose the truth of love." He was quite scandalized
at the manner in which St. Jerome treated Rufinus. Here
is his scathing comment: "I have read the letter which
you have written against Rufinus; and I confess, my dear
brother, it was with grief I read it, to see two persons,
once so united, now so animated against each other. . . .
If I could find you together in one place, I would cast
myself at your feet, in the transport of my grief and I
would conjure you both with tears, by what you owe to
yourselves, by what you owe to each other, and by what
you owe to the faithful, and particularly to the weak, for
whom Christ died, to whom you give on the theatre of
this life a spectacle so terrible and so pernicious — I would

conjure you, I say, not to publish writings in which there appears so much emotion against each other, writings which you cannot recall, and which, therefore may be a source of renewed hostility many years hence."

That is fraternal correction at its best — from a saint to a saint. St. Augustine, in his book *The City of God,* deals specifically with fraternal correction, in which he excoriates those Christians who, "through too much love of their good name and safety, through their fear of the deceits and violence of the wicked, through frailty and weakness, forbear to reproach the wicked when they have offended — they will not reprehend them, though herein they might reform some of them by this reprehensiveness."

There were giants in those early ages of the Church. Pope St. Fabian resisted the Emperor Philip, and would not allow him to partake of the sacraments until he had confessed and done penance; Pope St. Marcellus upbraided the Roman emperor, Maxentius, for his cruelty to the Christians. The emperor was so enraged that he had the Pope seized and sent into exile. How St. Ambrose fought the Emperor Theodosius is well known. "Thou hast followed David in his errors," said Ambrose, "now follow him in his repentance." The emperor at last accepted the fraternal correction and did true penance.

In the Middle Ages there was many a fine teacher of the art of admonition. Pope Innocent III addressed letters to all the faithful, reminding them that among the works of charity mentioned in Scripture is the recalling of the erring one from the path of his error.

St. Francis of Assisi never hesitated to correct when the occasion demanded, but he always was guided by his usual common sense and deep charity when he did it. The Lord, he said, wants conversions and not victims. That was his own guiding principle. He did not believe in excoriations. The way to convince a sinner of his sin, said he, was not to accuse him but to live in his presence in beauty and loving kindness. Look at your own soul first. "Let the brothers not pay attention to the sins of others, but rather let them recount their own in the bitterness of their soul." Not that he was silent when he saw evil — he gave everything its right name. He threatened the sinner with God's judgment. He was not always talking to the birds. One of his Rules was: "Blessed is the brother who is not eager to excuse himself, but who in humility is willing to be shamed and blamed, even if he has done nothing." Brother Elias was a thorn in his side. Francis often chided him for his pride, calling him "proud friar," and would turn aside so as not to speak to him, vainly seeking to correct him. Brother Bernard said to Francis, "I command you by holy obedience that every time we are together you rebuke and correct me harshly for my faults." Those Franciscans took correction in stride. Brother Juniper when he was reproved by his superior was not so much concerned over the humiliation as that the superior in reprehending him developed a sore throat. So Juniper went to the city and got materials to make a pottage of flour and butter to heal the throat.

But the greatest correctors of all time were St. Bridget of Sweden and St. Catherine of Siena, in their efforts to get the Popes to return from Avignon to Rome. Bridget did not mince words about the condition of the time. But she was a saint and was evidently inspired by God for the welfare of the Church.

But even a greater corrector was St. Catherine. We are likely to get the idea that she was a busybody, running about, blasting everyone, from the Popes down. Nothing is farther from the truth. Our Lord was her guide in all things. He had said to her, "You should all have compassion on each other and leave judgment to Me." He commanded her never to deliver a judgment in particular unless He had revealed it to her several times, but rather in general correct vices. So she said: "He who is perfect never judges the servants of God, nor any other creature whatsoever. Not even if with his own eyes he had seen others sinning should he pass judgment, but he should look upon them with compassion and plead before God, taking upon him the fault of his neighbor." There was no danger of Catherine being a detractor. She was sure of herself because she always sought to do the will of God. She made her "I will" the will of God. "Do God's will and mine," she wrote to the king. And to the Pope: "Fulfill the will of God and the ardent longing of my soul." To her the truth was evident and she felt obliged to proclaim it. She cared little whether she pleased or displeased, but she would allow no one to speak evil of priests. There was nothing of the heretic about Catherine of Siena.

She wrote to everybody — to prisoners, outcasts, nobles, businessmen, doctors, lawyers, kings, queens, cardinals, popes, and to common ordinary sinners. She even wrote to the pirate, John Hawkwood: "It is high time now that you thought a little of yourself and considered how great are the sufferings you have borne so long in serving the devil." She could wound, but it was always a wound of love.

One of her best letters of fraternal correction was the one to her niece in religion, about a certain danger: "For if I were to know or hear it, even if I were much farther away than I am, I would give you such a discipline that it would stay in your memory all your whole life, never mind who may be by."

The Brothers of the Common Life, to which Thomas à Kempis belonged, had this rule: "To give and receive fraternal correction and admonition from one another." Thomas à Kempis has little to say about fraternal correction, very likely because, writing for religious, he knew that their rules were enough. But in one passage he shows his usual common sense and good theology. He writes: "If, after being admonished once or twice, a person does not amend, do not argue with him, but commend the whole matter to God, that His will and honor may be furthered in all His servants, for God knows well how to turn evil to good." "Patience!" he teaches. If you cannot correct your own faults, why be so impatient about the faults of others? Father Florentius, of the same Community, said, "when you accuse another, be pitiful as to a weak brother." Another priest of that community, Father John Gronde, used to preach six hours at a time. That is fraternal correction with a vengeance!

St. Francis de Sales preached gentleness in correction, honey and not vinegar. When Louise de Marillac complained that sometimes she was not severe enough, St. Vincent said to her: "If the gentleness of your character requires an admixture of vinegar, borrow a little from the example of Our Divine Savior." But Louise rarely used vinegar in her doses of fraternal correction. When she corrected, she encouraged.

It is always refreshing to hear St. Teresa discuss any matter. She never lost her fine sense of humor. She understood human nature, and always allowed for it. She did not believe in correcting people to death. "The Lord deliver me," she said, "from people who are so spiritual that, cost what it may, they want to bring everybody to perfect contemplation." Again she said: "It is amusing to see souls, who, while they are at prayer, fancy they are willing to be despised and publicly insulted for the love of God, yet afterwards do all they can to hide their small defects; if anyone unjustly accuses them of a fault, God deliver us from their outcries."

Teresa concluded sadly that the language of correction was no longer in use, and "even preachers go about arranging their sermons so as to displease no one." But she never minimized. She even reprimanded King Philip II, to whom she used to refer jokingly as "my friend the king." "Remember, Sire," she said to him once, "that Saul was anointed and yet he was rejected." Yet he had the highest respect for her, even though she revealed to him his most secret thoughts.

There would be no end of citing examples of the science of fraternal correction as practised by the saints. They knew their own weaknesses — to us it seems they exaggerated them — hence had sympathy for others, a spiritual mercy that moved them to reclaim souls. They had the sense of honest humility. A Spanish ecclesiastic once published a bitter pasquinade against Pope Pius V, and because of it was condemned by the civil magistrates. But the Pope sent for him, and said to him forgivingly, "My friend, when in future you see any defect in my conduct, I pray you to warn me of it, that I may correct myself." It took a saintly man to say that. We are not saints. But we are not freed from the obligation of giving and receiving fraternal correction. It may be that in our condition we are rarely bound to correct our neighbor. But if we cultivate a true love for our neighbor and are interested in his salvation, when the need arises for us to give to him the merciful alms of admonition, the Holy Ghost will show us how to do it in all brotherly love. God will work through us to preach the Gospel of salvation. But whether or not we are able to give correction, we can at least be willing to receive it. That is not the least of the heroisms. The man who shows us our faults, no matter what his motive may be, is our best friend, if we only knew it. He may be the instrument of God for our salvation. Strange, if while he probes our wound and we wince under the pain and resent it, he may be receiving the blessing of God for doing unto us the greatest possible act of mercy.

Mother of Mercy, Refuge of Sinners, admonish us, and pray for us!

Chapter XIII

To Instruct the Ignorant

THE instruction of the ignorant must hold a prominent place in any religion. Even the false religions, when concerning themselves with ideas which a man cannot find out for himself, have relied almost entirely upon the power of teaching. But, depending upon the vagaries of human teaching alone, false religions go further and further into the extravagances of error.

True religion, true Revelation, however, guided by the infallible spirit of God, manifests itself by the instrumentality of man. Revelations to individuals are rarely made. We must depend for the knowledge of the truth upon those whom God inspires to teach, or to whom He imparts the office and the power. What is the Old Testament but God's primer for His children? And the Gospel, the Evangel, is but the "Good news," the solid course of instruction for those who seek the Kingdom of God.

Throughout the Old Testament you will find insistence upon the duty of instructing in the ways of God, and the beauty of that office. The Book of Proverbs could be quoted indefinitely. There are many variations of the command, "To give subtilty to little ones, to the young man knowledge and understanding" (1:4). "Be not ashamed to inform the unwise and foolish, and the aged, that are judged by young men: and thou shalt be well instructed in all things, and well approved in the sight of all men living" (Ecclus. 42:8). Over and over is given the order: Instruct thy son.

But it is in the New Testament that the duty of instructing the ignorant becomes of supreme importance. Our Lord set the sublime example as Teacher. He is the Light, "the true light, that enlightens every man who comes into the world" (John 1:9). "I am the light of the world" (*Ibid.* 8:12). Not only was He the Light, but He commanded His apostles to be a light, too. "You are the light of the world . . . let your light shine before men" (Matt. 5:14–16). And His commission to them was, "Go forth and teach all nations."

St. Paul insisted to Timothy that a bishop be "a teacher" (1 Tim. 3:3), "ready to teach" (2 Tim. 2:25). "Command and teach these things" (1 Tim. 4:11). Preaching and teaching — that was the chief concern of the apostles, to bring the knowledge of Divine truth to the ignorant. For that reason it was the most eminent work of charity in the Church, and it is plain to see how when theology became systematized, instruction was included among the works of mercy, including as it did not only the general work of official teaching, but the duty of meeting the needs of the individual in regard to a particular enlightenment. This latter was a personal rather than an official duty. But even in that sense every Christian shared in the office of apostle.

So the Church, even before there was any system of works of mercy, always busied herself about the instruction of the ignorant. The countless tomes of the Fathers were but evidence of compliance with that particular work of mercy: instructing the ignorant, and opposing those who preached error in order to lead astray the unknowing. "Instruct in the truth of God," was ever their motto. And that has been always the fundamental idea with the Church from first to last in education.

It was just there that Christianity made a tremendous change in the educational system, if you can call it a system, which it found in the pagan world. Godly education was insisted upon, of course, among the Jews. At the time of our Lord the child was instructed not only by its father and mother — it was the father's work chiefly — but also in the schools connected with the synagogues. That education was chiefly, almost solely, religious.

But in the pagan concept of life at that time there was no concern to educate a child except in reference to its future citizenship. The child was a member of the state, first, last and always. Nazi ideas are not new in the world. Now the Church took that idea and spiritualized it, and began with the proposition which ever since has been at the bottom of Christian education: that a Christian child must be educated in view of his citizenship in the Kingdom of God.

The pagan education in Rome was even more citizen-conscious, more practical and prosy than in Greece. There were no public schools, elementary schools, as we understand them. A boy was taught to read, but the greater part of his instruction consisted in manly exercise, in processes which fitted him for contact with a military world, similar to much modern pedagogical tyranny, with very little interest in the development of the intellect and none whatever in the culture of the soul. It was, we know, the age of "Bread and Circuses," the quest of material prosperity and the consequent opportunity to have fun. So that when Christianity came to Rome, it found a decadent civilization, more than half slave, wholly materialistic. We do not minimize Roman culture. There was much of it, as is evident from the innumerable classics, and that in itself indicates much popular education, for you do not pick up masterpieces out of the street. Whatever that learning was, the Church, right from the beginning, took hold of it and made it her own. Not only did she insist upon the importance of education at home, but she provided opportunities in the churches.

The Church rarely destroys; she transforms if it is at

all possible to do so. Hence if we have the pagan classics today, it is due to the Church that protected and saved them, and to the monks who transcribed them. The Fathers of the Church, who had been well trained in the classics — like St. Augustine for one — never scorned them but used them as a means to convey knowledge of the Gospel, and kept them as a part, a very substantial part, in the furtherance of Christian culture. St. Jerome, for instance, in the judgment of scholars, wrote better Latin than Cicero.

In those days a bishop was not only a bishop, he was also a schoolmaster. Even the Popes found time to teach children. Gregory the Great, for example, established a school of music near the Lateran. For centuries after his death there could be seen the bed upon which he reclined while teaching singing when he was ill, and the whip with which he corrected any recalcitrant pupil. Indeed, every homily preached by the Fathers was a course of instruction. You cannot infer from the work of a genius that every contemporary of his was a genius, too. But genius does not spring up miraculously, and the presence of so many great scholars, great culturists, great educators among the early teachers — and we have but a fraction of the works produced — indicates that the standards of the populace, from which these geniuses sprang, were, indeed, very high.

Nobly, then, did the Church from the beginning obey the Divine injunction to instruct the ignorant. These men labored to spread the Gospel, and that — even today, in spite of all the vagaries of so-called learning and culture — is the very essence of true education.

It is not in our province to discuss the history of education. But there are broad lines, which, if followed, indicate the perpetual interest of the Church in instructing the ignorant. It could not be otherwise. To the Church it was a vital work. It is evident when, for instance, you compare the bright Catholic Africa of Augustine's time with the darkness which came by the invasion of the barbarians. Schools for the public disappeared with everything else; and if it had not been for the monasteries which quietly carried on the work, there would have remained no education whatsoever. It is that era of darkness which demonstrates, more than anything else, the importance of Ireland in the Divine plan. Scarcely converted from paganism, it so speedily spiritualized its traditional culture, and went at Christian learning with such a rush, by the intensive cultivation of the monastic life, that it soon became the land of saints and scholars, and burned with zeal to carry the torch of faith and learning to less fortunate lands. There is some innate desire for learning in the soul of an Irishman. When the light mainly passed from Ireland, by invasion and later on by the religious persecutions of Reformation times, the Irishman held fast to his educational traditions as best he could, crouching behind the hedges to learn, and ready, when opportunity did come, to give to his children in America and other lands where he found hospitality the blessings of an education. No sacrifice was too great to bring instruction to the ignorant. Historically one could justly say that this spiritual work of mercy was a peculiarly Irish one.

This fact must not be forgotten when you consider how the monastic schools saved Christian education, and in those days the only education was the education permeated by religion.

With the revival of education under Charlemagne you will find it almost entirely in schools connected with the palace, the bishop's house, and the monastery. The hospitals had their schools, too, and the later Guilds, which seemed to include in their program all the works of mercy, took a great interest in the education of the children of the members. Education was pretty general. In speaking of the monastic schools, one is apt to get the idea that they were solely schools for the monks. In that sense "monastic" would be something of a misnomer; for the monastic schools were in reality public schools, or more like our own parochial schools. They taught the monks, the novices, but even in a larger manner they catered to the children in the vicinity. It was not an occasional oasis. You cannot get blood out of a stone; and the medieval learning, so broad that it is staggering to contemplate, with its production of immense Christian libraries, implies a correspondingly large audience. Books are written to be read, and a book is not worth writing unless it has a worth-while public. The striking thing about medieval learning is that it put first things first; that while it gave a tremendous amount of time to the liberal arts, to philosophical inquiry, it never lost sight of its chief aim, to instruct for citizenship in the Kingdom of God.

There seemed to be no limit to the education to which a boy could aspire. It was not a mere smattering of indeterminate knowledge, such as too many of the universities of today are content with providing — rejecting about everything else as well as the knowledge of God — but it was a solid system, developing of necessity into the higher learning of the great Catholic universities. In the thirteenth century, though long before that great schools were common, education was not merely preparatory, for men continued to study up to the age of thirty or forty. And, strange, the more learned men became, the more they loved to teach the ignorant. The great Doctor, Gerson, loved to surround himself with little children, to teach them their catechism. The learning in those days was scholastic education at its best. And it was not a closed corporation. The thousands of students attending the many universities are proof that learning was not confined to the few favored but was for the poor scholar as well.

The Church never forgot that education was a spir-

itual alms. It was motivated chiefly by religion. If religion
failed, education failed, because charity failed. That was
the double disaster of the Reformation. The monasteries,
as we said before, were the patrimony of the poor. When
they were confiscated by the greedy nobles, when the endowments were poured into private coffers, there was no
longer support for the free schools, and as for institutions
of higher learning, what sense in keeping them going
when the system they taught — that hated scholasticism —
would be a continual reproach to those who had rifled the
treasury of the Church. The Reformation set education
back hundreds of years. We have not yet recovered from
the blow in those countries where its false principles were
adopted. Luckily, rather providentially, all was not destroyed everywhere. The countries which remained loyally
Catholic continued the Catholic system, bettered it. The
Counter-Reformation was not slow to see that there must
be made a superhuman effort to scatter the darkness which
men had brought upon the world when they quenched
the torch of faith in so many lands, and to revive inten-
sively the work of mercy by instructing the ignorant in the
truths of God. The Providence of God is always at hand.
The Church cannot fail. And surely, looking at the matter
historically, the rise of the Jesuits and their contribution
to the cause of education at the time when the world
needed it most is one of the astounding facts of history.
The prime reason for the establishment of many orders
and communities in the Church, outside the chief one of
personal sanctification, was the instruction of youth. But
that duty of instructing was never confined to the pro-
fessionally educated, whether teacher or writer. Every
saint is a specialist in the work of mercy, since all the
works of mercy are but the practical manifestation of the
spirit of Christ in His Church.

St. Francis de Sales was a busy bishop, but in spite of
that, rather because of that, he was forever instructing.

Numberless were the heretics he instructed back and prayed back into the Church, and numberless are the souls he is still instructing by his spiritual books. St. Jane Frances de Chantal used to say that he was born to instruct men, and then she added, "Father De Condren was born to instruct angels." St. Francis himself said: "It is a good means to become learned, for a man to study hard; a better to have a learned master; and the best of all to teach others."

St. Vincent de Paul tells a beautiful story of a poor country girl, Marguerite Naseau, who had joined the Daughters of Charity. As a girl, she could not even read, but somehow she got the idea that she ought to teach children. She could not go to school, so she bought a primer, or alphabet, and when she got time off from her work she would go to the pastor or his assistant. She asked what the first four letters were, and then went home to study them out. Thus she went through all the letters until she mastered them. While she herded the cattle, she studied her little book, and when anyone passed she would stop him and say, "Sir, would you please tell me how to pronounce this word." When she finally had learned to read, she began to teach the little girls of her own village, and then went from one village to another on the same errand of mercy. She was half starved, slept in the fields, worked night and day for the sake of the girls. She gave away everything she got, persevered against all odds, though she was ridiculed and even slandered. At last she came to St. Vincent and offered herself for his work of charity. Strange, she became the first Sister of Charity. There is no finer example of the fulfillment of the command to instruct the ignorant than that of Marguerite Naseau.

The sixteenth century was productive of an endless supply of Catholic educators. It was because there was need — and God always supplies the need. St. Angela

Merici (1474–1540), the foundress of the Ursulines, had been convinced that a crying need of the times was a better education in the fundamentals of Christianity for young girls. She began humbly, seeing her personal obligation to do the works of mercy in this special branch, so she simply turned her home into a little school. The lowly venture ended with the establishment of the great Ursulines, the first order of teaching women, at Brescia, in 1535. St. Joseph Calasanctius (1556–1648) founding the Piarists for the instruction of children; Julie Billiart, at seven years of age explaining the catechism to her little playmates, and later founding the Sisters of Notre Dame de Namur; Madame Barat, one of the great educators; Mother Seton, the real foundress of the parochial school system in the United States: these are but a few names, chosen almost at random, of holy women who became convinced that the instruction of the ignorant is a sublime vocation, and who gave their lives to that work of mercy.

Somehow we are apt to take our educational system for granted, to think that it just grew naturally, but in believing that, we lose sight of the great souls who fought the initial battles.

No praise is too great for St. John Baptist de la Salle. Looking back at him now, we see that he was the most advanced educator in the eighteenth century, certainly one of the greatest educational reformers in all history. And again you might say that his educational career was almost accidental. Better to say it was one of those sudden manifestations of the Providence of God. It was a time when many of the clergy and laity were deeply interested in getting a solid Christian education for the ordinary people.

Prominent among them was a Monsieur Nyel, of Rouen, who had the work of training teachers. De la Salle, then a priest and a Canon, being a close friend of Nyel, became interested in educational work. It soon became a fine obsession with him, and he determined to make it his life's work. He resigned his Canonry, gave up his private fortune, which was considerable, and threw himself heart and soul into teaching the poor who could not pay for an education. One great departure he made was to do away with the teaching of Latin in elementary education, up to that time compulsory, and to build up the education of the poor, who had no need of Latin, upon their native language. Thus he has ever been regarded as the real founder of the modern system of primary education.

It would be impossible merely to catalogue the religious communities which carry on the torch of learning. The glory of the Church today are the thousands of sisters and brothers, not to say priests, who make our Catholic schools possible. Their work is a perpetual wonder, while in it they sanctify themselves by devotion to a work of mercy which must be considered of primary importance to the Heart of Christ, who said, "Suffer the little children to come unto me."

Not all of us can be practical teachers. Most of us are always learners, never smart enough to be teachers. But it is very much within our province, nevertheless, to participate in the exercise of the spiritual work of mercy, to instruct the ignorant. Even in our limited social circle there are many occasions where, out of our meager knowledge we can instruct others. Even a chance conversation may lead to the Kingdom of God, if we know how to explain our Catholic beliefs. We all are obliged to be apostles. There would be far more conversions of non-Catholics, if we took to heart our obligation to instruct others.

But in daily Catholic life there is no lack of opportunity. We have our Catholic schools to carry on, a double burden of taxation if there ever was one. But they are well worth all the sacrifices we make to keep them going, doing the work of Christ. There are our Sunday schools, where parish schools are impossible. In them many a Catholic man and woman can find opportunity for true zeal. There is the Society for the Propagation of the Faith, the Holy Childhood, all the missionary activities which are so numerous today and so much in need of our help. There are our Catholic papers, magazines, books, which are defending our Catholic cause. We need more Catholic writers.

Our whole Catholic life is evangelical. It presupposes teaching. "Go, teach all nations."

For that reason there is no more important work of mercy than to instruct others unto the knowledge of Him who is the Way and the Truth.

Mother of Mercy, Seat of Wisdom, pray for us!

Chapter XIV

To Counsel the Doubtful

OFTENTIMES it is hard to mark off the virtues and confine them within certain defined compartments. There is a great deal of overlapping in the Christian soul. Rather might it be said that its garment is woven of one piece. Thus it may seem strange that Counsel figures both in the Gifts of the Holy Ghost and in the spiritual works of mercy. Only you will note that in these cases Counsel is viewed from different angles. The Gift of Counsel is primarily a gift we receive, while Counsel in the works of mercy is more properly a gift we make. There is, of course, in both of them something passive and something active. You cannot give counsel to others unless you are equipped to do so, and for that proper equipment you must have been counseled by the Holy Ghost. So that — it is a tremendous thought, a humbling thought — when you counsel others you are acting with the Holy Ghost, for the Holy Ghost. You are acting as God; you are partner with God. You have consulted with Him, advised with Him, and as a junior partner you take over the case from Him, the Senior Counsel, and give the advice where it is needed. You are appointed by the Court of Heaven to act as lawyer for a poor man, for you are giving spiritual alms to him. You could develop that thought, indeed, in all the works of mercy, since the only efficacy they have lies in the fact that they are done to your neighbor for the love of God. Unless they are done by you as a member of the firm of God and Company, they have no official value. It is all a manifestation of the great truth of the Mystical Body.

The Scriptures insist upon the obligation of giving counsel. What was the purpose of all the inspired word but to give counsel? Every prophet was par excellence an adviser to Israel in happy days and in trying days. The Book of Proverbs and Ecclesiasticus, for example, give counsel in every line. And as all the writers of the inspired books are counselors, they urge upon others its beauty, its necessity. The Psalmist, for instance, speaking of the widespread corruption before the Incarnation when the fool said in his heart "There is no God," condemns the evil man for his inability or unwillingness to give proper counsel: "You have confounded the counsel of the poor man, but the Lord is his hope" (13:6). God condemns those who have neglected His advice: "You have despised all my counsel, and have neglected my reprehensions" (Prov. 1:25), counsel that was usually given by holy men sealed by God for that office. So the Wise Man goes on: "Designs are brought to nothing where there is no counsel; but where there are many counselors, they are established" (15:22). Again: "A brother that is helped by his brother is like a strong city" (18:19). "Hear counsel, and receive instructions, that thou mayest be wise in the latter end" (19:20).

"Counsel in the heart of a man is like deep water; but a wise man will draw it out" (20:5). It is the mark of wisdom to take counsel: "Give ear, my son, and take counsel, and cast not away my advice" (Ecclus. 6:24).

Running all though the Book of Job is the condemnation of evil counsel, of the pretended comforters who were not fit to give him advice. Even the patient Job resented the unqualified interference in the state of his soul. "And I wish that you would hold your peace, that you might be thought to be wise men" (13:5); and Tobias, while declar-

ing that the Counsel of God "is not in man's power,"
advises his son: "Seek counsel always of a wise man"
(4:19).

But the Spirit of Counsel dominates the New Testament. "Counselor" was one of the titles given to the
Messias by Isaias: "and his name shall be called Wonderful, Counsellor, God the Mighty, the Father of the World
to come, the Prince of Peace" (9:6). "And, the spirit of the
Lord shall rest upon him . . . the spirit of counsel" (11:2).

The Prophets, as we have said, were primarily counselors, often tenderly pleading, often accusing and condemning, but always with a view to the glory of God and
the salvation of their hearers. The line of prophets continues, from the Old to the New Dispensation. The New
Testament opens with a prophet, John the Baptist, counseling the doubtful in an upset era, setting right those
who were looking for the Messias. But the voice of John,
of all the prophets indeed, was a voice crying in the
wilderness. There could be only one true Counselor, the
Divine One. To repeat His counsels would be to quote
every word of His narrated by the Evangelists. His office
was essentially to teach, to advise, not only in a general
way but even in particularly personal circumstances. He
was eager to give counsel whenever it was asked, and even
when it was not asked. Sometimes, as in the case of the
rich young man who went away sad, His advice was not
taken; but He tried, His compassionate soul always eager
to help. There is for us a lesson in that sad story. Sometimes we feel the holy urge to give counsel, even though
the case may seem hopeless. We must do our duty and give
the counsel anyway. It may bear fruit later on. We are not
told what became of the rich young man. Perhaps he did
take the advice and became a great saint before he died.
We are kept guessing about his fate. Anyway the Lord
had counseled, and much good came of it to many who
have read the story. There were so many who were doubt-

ful in the days of our Lord — even His Apostle Thomas was to doubt — that much of His time was taken up in counseling them, in dissipating their doubts, Every miracle of His was a counsel. All His works of mercy are, indeed, counsels, advising His followers to look to Him as the Great Exemplar of mercy and to imitate Him. "Inasmuch as ye have done it to them, ye have done it unto me," is His divine counsel of the works of mercy.

The greatest counselor after Christ was St. Paul. He was always solving doubts. What are his Epistles but the effort to set things right in the hearts of the followers of the Lord. "Exhort one another every day," he wrote to the Hebrews (3:13). It was the same with all the apostles; with all the Fathers of the Church; with all the bishops and priests; with all the spiritual writers; with all the confessors; with all the theologians, dogmatic, moral, and ascetic: all were, and are, the dispensers of the wisdom of the Divine Counselor.

Every saint is a spiritual lawyer. He is so filled with the gift of counsel that he is ready on the instant to further his Father's business by advising those who cannot think straight because their minds are twisted by the cares of life. Sinners need the light because they are in a complete blackout. The one thing about the saint is that he is no respecter of persons. Advice is needed, and he gives it whether it is wanted or not. The story is told of the great charity worker, St. John the Almoner, who advised Nicetas, the Governor, against imposing a heavy tax, which would be a grievous burden, especially on the poor. The Governor, in anger, left him. St. John then merely sent this message to Nicetas: "The sun is going to set." It was enough. The Governor changed his mind.

The saint was good at giving advice because he was good at taking it. "When you have learned my dangers," wrote St. Bernard, "favor me with your advice and prayers." Unlike most of us he wanted advice, not approval. "They who praise me," he said, "truly reproach and confound me." This same saint did not feel the impulse to run around giving advice. In the preface to his book, "On the Love of God," dedicated to the Cardinal Chancellor of Rome, he wrote: "You were accustomed to ask prayers of me and not questions, yet, indeed, I feel certain that I am equipped for neither."

A beautiful thing about the spiritual friendship of St. Francis and St. Clare was that they were mutual advisers. From the beginning of the Franciscan movement she counseled him, and he her. He promised her that he and his friars would always give help to her and her sisters. When Pope Gregory IX was in any need he would write to Clare for prayers and advice, and at once he felt comforted and at peace. Again, the Franciscan idea was not to throw out advice indiscriminately. Francis never gave advice to others which he had not first followed himself. He practised what he preached. Words were of the least importance to him. Once a learned Dominican said to Brother Leo: "I know many, good Father, that be in mortal sin to whom I do not speak to warn them of their impiety; will their souls therefore be required at my hands?" Francis, to whom the difficulty was submitted, replied that the servant of God should so burn and shine forth by life and holiness in himself, that by the light of of his example and by the speech of his holy conversation he should reprove all the impious. "Thus, say I," he continued, "his splendor and the odor of his fame will announce to all their iniquities." Pretty good advice. Words may move, but examples draw.

We saw elsewhere that St. Catherine was pastmaster in the difficult science of fraternal correction. But those were the high lights in her career, striking because they dealt with world affairs; but the far greater part of her life was devoted to the humdrum work of counseling unknown individuals. Not all of them unknown, for even Popes humbly sought her advice, and waited upon her "I will." But generally she exercised her work of counseling in teaching ordinary people who came to her at all hours for advice. She never turned them away, but advised them, and then, to seal the advice, would pray for them during the night, and even take the discipline for them. The advice she gave to others cost her dear.

There was no saint more eager to get advice or give it than St. Teresa. She always took advice, she obeyed her superiors even when she felt they were mistaken. "How many people go astray in the world," she wrote, "for want of seeking guidance, especially in what affects their neighbor's interests." There was a nobleman of Ávila, Francesco de Salcedo, whom she consulted about her visions and other supernatural favors. He told her that they came from the devil. He was a poor counselor, but he was honest. But the point is that even St. Teresa felt that a layman could exercise the spiritual work of mercy, and counsel the doubtful. Salcedo, after the death of his wife, became a priest, and was chaplain at the Ávila convent.

Teresa was a sane counselor. Her brother Lorenzo was very holy. He had sent gifts to Teresa, and in return she sent him a hair shirt! But with it went good advice. She wrote: "God prefers your health and obedience to your penances." She was always advising her nuns against useless or morbid mortification. She would give small presents to the learned theologians whom she consulted about her soul. "I like to be independent with these gentlemen," she said, "so that I can speak my mind to them." Indeed, she must have been a wonderful adviser. St. John of the Cross used to carry in a shabby pouch the letters she had written him, together with the Holy Scriptures. They were his mainstay on every journey. But he obtained so much comfort from the letters, that one day he became scrupulous and burned the lot. Speaking of Ávila, the conversion of St. John of God and of St. Francis Borgia was the result of the preaching of Blessed John of Ávila, the Apostle of Andalusia.

St. Francis de Sales had the right idea of giving counsel. He regarded his congregation as composed of individuals. He would preach in the smallest chapels, and if only two or three people were present, he would feel well repaid. He never was a wrangler. As we know, he trusted in honey rather than in vinegar. Bossuet used the same message. "Heretics," he said, "must be won by a display of charity rather than by wrangling with them; the zeal of a disputant may possibly spring from his desire for victory. A man may feel bitter towards you when you attack his ideas, but he will always be grateful to those who are anxious for his welfare. He is on his guard against being regarded as the spoils of victory, but he will never be annoyed at being loved."

We are told that St. Philip Neri used to wander about Rome, entering into conversation with everybody he met. He won their confidence, and then advised them. He was always the true gentleman.

The Abbé Huvelin, as famous a confessor as the Curé d'Ars, never repulsed anyone who came looking for his advice. But he did not rely upon words. He said: "We do good much less by what we say or do than by what we are." When Charles de Foucaud, his penitent, wanted to found a religious order, the Abbé said of his proposed Rule: "It is an impossible rule, containing everything else except discretion." The same Abbé said: "A young man has no idea of the influence he may exercise over others by giving them an example of purity combined with strength and courage." Good example is the best counsel.

We are not saints, but that does not excuse us from being counselors for the Lord, and with the Lord; junior counsel, as it were. In our daily life, besides the times when our advice is asked, there are many opportunities to give salutary counsel. There would be far more conversions of non-Catholics, for instance, if the ordinary Catholic would recognize the fact that he should be an apostle ready to counsel in the difficulties proposed to him.

Then, too, there is many a sin that would be averted among our friends if we took our courage in hand and kindly pointed out the folly of a proposed action. That does not mean that we should run about advising the world, feeling that everybody but ourselves is out of step. There is no bore like the one that is always saying, "Now if you ask *my* advice." Better to wait till you are asked. Better, on the other hand, to seek advice for yourself, and not have the conviction that nobody can tell you anything. The easy swapping of advice is the sign of a true friendship.

The works of mercy are a command to all of us. We do not need to be learned theologians to exercise any of them. They are the people's charter. All we need to have in order to exercise them is the good will. The Holy Ghost will do the rest.

Mother of Mercy, Our Lady of Good Counsel, pray for us!

Chapter XV

To Comfort the Sorrowful

ONE of the most beautiful lines in all the Scriptures is the prophecy of St. John the Evangelist in regard to the elect — "And God will wipe away every tear from their eyes (Apoc. 7:17). That is so thoroughly in keeping with the loving heart of the beloved disciple, who was always preaching the gospel of love, and, infinitely more in keeping with the merciful heart of Jesus Christ, Love itself.

Not only did the Old Testament prophesy that the Messias would be the Comforter and Consoler, par excellence, but God in His revelation ordered that man should be a comfort to his neighbor. The hundreds of texts commanding help to the poor might all be grouped under the heading *Comfort*, as indeed, they do serve to point every work of mercy. "He hath not forgotten the cry of the poor" (Ps. 9:13) would serve as the eulogy of every true follower of Christ. It is the tribute which Shakespeare gives to Henry IV.

> He hath a tear for pity and a hand
> Open as day for melting charity.

Sometimes "tears are near the eye," as the old Irish have it, but tears, too, may well up from the bottom of the heart, out of sympathy for the afflicted friend. When the Prophet Eliseus was about to raise to life the child of the Sunamite woman he showed that his heart grieved for her. What pity in his words! "Let her alone for her soul is in anguish" (4 Kings 4:27).

Poor afflicted Job cried out for comfort: "Have pity on me, have pity on me, at least you my friends, because the hand of the Lord hath touched me" (19:21). There are so many today, like him, crying for comfort. If we would only realize how much we can do to alleviate their distress. Even a word of sympathy has a world of healing. The Book of Proverbs repeats this message many times: "He that is inclined to mercy shall be blessed" (22:9). "By mercy and faith sins are purged away" (15:27). And this mercy was not only the giving of food and drink. Of far greater importance was the pitying love for which every soul hungers.

But when the real comforter, Jesus Christ, came to earth, bringing with Him redemption, it was then only that true consolation was brought to the afflicted. Isaias had foretold of Him that, "the bruised reed he shall not break, and smoking flax he shall not quench" (42:3) He found much sorrow to be ministered to. Every miracle of healing which He did was to comfort the sorrowful. When death came, as in the case of the son of the widow of Naim, and of Lazarus, He was there, even before He worked the miracles of raising, to comfort the dear ones of the departed. Twice Jesus wept, once on the death of Lazarus, and then over His beloved Jerusalem. St. Gregory Nazianzen says that Jesus wept so that henceforth tears might be laudable. St. John tells us that when Lazarus died many of the Jews came to comfort Martha and Mary. But what poor comfort beside the presence of Jesus!

Not only was He comforter on earth, but when it was necessary that He return to His Father, His great promise was that He would send the permanent comforter, the Holy Ghost: "and your sorrow shall be turned into joy" (John 16:20). The beautiful office of Christ as comforter, and of the Holy Ghost as comforter, occupied such a place in the Gospels, that it is clear why, in imitation of these Divine Exemplars, the very important duty of comforting the sorrowful was recognized early as a work of mercy incumbent upon the Christian. St. Paul, the Apostle of Charity, can also be called the Apostle of Comfort. Over and over he insists upon it as a Christian duty. "Blessed be the God and Father of our Lord Jesus Christ, the Father of mercies and the God of all comfort, who comforts us in all our afflictions that we also may be able to comfort those who are in any distress by the comfort wherewith we ourselves are comforted by God. For as the sufferings of Christ abound in us, so also through Christ does our comfort abound. For whether we are afflicted, it is for your instruction and salvation; or whether we are comforted, it is for your comfort; which shows its efficacy in the endurance of the selfsame sufferings that we also suffer. And our hope for you is steadfast, knowing that as you are partakers of the sufferings, so will you also be of the comfort" (2 Cor. 1:3–7).

"But God who comforts the humble, comforted us by the arrival of Titus" (2 Cor. 7:6); "Brethren, be comforted" (2 Cor. 13:11); "We have accordingly found comfort in you, brethren, amid all our trials and tribulations, on account of your faith" (1 Thess. 3:7); "Comfort one another with these words" (1 Thess. 4:18). These are but a few of the texts where St. Paul preaches the beauty of consolation. And St. Peter urges his flock to be "compassionate, lovers of the brethren" (1 Pet. 3:8).

Every Christian necessarily had the conviction of sin. He was in sorrow for that reason. He could look only to the Redeemer for comfort in his misery. And as he found all his consolation in Jesus, so was he eager to share that consolation with his brethren. St. Thomas defines mercy as sorrow over the sufferings of others, and, if there is real sorrow, there must follow the effort to relieve those sufferings, either by removing the cause of them, or by comforting him who has to endure them. The very word "comfort," meaning to be strong together, indicates that. It is the giving of part of your own strength to help your neighbor to endure. It is indeed true that misery loves company. To sympathize is to share another's pain. Sorrow may be a fine remedy at times, but in itself it is negative. It may be even a fatal weakness. St. John Chrysostom considered sadness and dejection of spirit, "the worst of human evils, a perpetual domestic rack, a darkness and tempest of the mind, an interior war, a distemper which consumes the vigor of the soul, and impairs all her faculties." Again, he calls it, "the most intolerable torment of the soul, a grief beyond all expression, a punishment more cruel than all punishments." St. Bernard therefore says: "The Holy Ghost cannot suffer the odious sadness of the children of the world to remain in the soul of His servants."

But even that sadness, when it was concerned about others, could be a great power. "My weapons against the enemies of God," said St. Ambrose, "are my tears; with these alone can the priest protect himself. I cannot and may not do otherwise."

You will find that gift of compassion in all the saints. It is told of St. Peter the Exorcist that when he was released from prison he was commanded to comfort his fellow prisoners. "Weep with the unhappy," was the motto of St. Columban. St. Basil was so gentle and sympathetic with the weak that he was accused of softness and a leaning to error. St. Athanasius was obliged to defend him against the charge. St. Benedict was called "Founder of Peace," because of his great sympathy.

It is told of St. Bernard that though he was stern and fiery by nature, and very severe with himself, he was always seized with feelings of intense compassion at the sight of pain or weakness, or moral or physical infirmity in others. He could not attend the funeral of a stranger even without weeping. That kindness and sympathy he showed even to animals. If he saw a hare pursued by dogs, or a small bird in danger of being caught by a bird of prey, he was so full of compassion that he could not help making the Sign of the Cross in the air to ensure the safety of the dumb creatures. We have already seen the tenderness which St. Francis showed to all the creatures of God. Kindness was a Franciscan trait. St. Francis, and St. Dominic, too, used to weep at their neighbor's necessities when they could not relieve them.

One of the loveliest passages in Scripture is found in Jonas (4:11). Jonas was displeased that Ninive had not been destroyed. But the Lord said to him: "And shall not I spare Ninive, that great city, in which there are more than a hundred and twenty thousand persons that know not how to distinguish between their right hand and their left, and many beasts?"

St. Claire, too, radiated sympathy. If she saw any of her sisters troubled with anger or sadness she called them to her and comforted them. If she made a gift, a smile went with it. She diffused joy. She was known as the "gracious daughter of the Scefi." Pope Alexander IV called her, "The Princess of the Poor," "the Dutchess of the Humble." She was the incarnation of Lady Courtesy.

One of the Franciscan friars, Brother Gregory, was sent to travel through all the provinces, in order "to console the brethren."

It was so, too, with St. Catherine of Siena. Well was she called "Catherine the Consoler." Her whole mission in life was to strengthen others, from the pope down. Pope Urban said of her: "You see how this little woman confounds us. She is confident, and we doubt; and she strengthens us with her holy persuasions." Some of the most beautiful incidents in her life concern her comforting of the poor condemned criminals. As we have seen, she brightened their last hours, and sent them to their death comforted and full of trust in the mercy of God.

St. Francis of Sales was so sympathetic because he had learned the lesson in the hard way. At one time in his life he thought he was damned. But that terrible trial made him sympathetic with the sufferings of others. St. Jane Frances de Chantal had gone through a like period of darkness, but it gave her a big heart, to feel for others who were going through the same temptations.

It must have taken the sting out of poverty and suffering to be helped by St. Vincent de Paul and his Daughters of Charity, so comforting was their manner of doing kindness. The white coronet has long been the symbol of consolation the world over. Dearly did the Sisters earn their glorious name of "Angels of the Battlefield." How beautifully the Orientals have called them, "the swallows of Allah."

It is this spirit of comfort which is at the bottom of all the many religious societies founded to rescue the fallen. It was to bring consolation, new hope, new love, and to destroy despairing fear. "Fear must not stifle love," said Pascal, but the aim of the works of mercy is to cause love to stifle fear.

To comfort the sorrowful is to restore life to them, to dissipate the clouds and show that God's sun is still shining. It is to win the soul to God. One of St. Teresa's maxims was: "Accommodate yourself to everyone's humor; be cheerful with the happy, grave with the sad, — in short, be all to all, that you may win all."

Just there is the heart of the spiritual work of mercy — to comfort the sorrowful. It is to wipe the blinding tears out of their eyes, so that they may behold the True Comforter. One of our Lady's most lovely titles is "Comforter of the Afflicted." Standing at the foot of the Cross, she comforted her Divine Son. She is always standing beneath the shadow of a Cross. This time she is standing at our Cross, waiting to take us down from it when our agony is over, to lead us home to the land of eternal consolation.

Mother of Mercy, Comforter of the Afflicted, pray for us!

Chapter XVI

To Bear Wrongs Patiently

AT FIRST sight there seems to be a difficulty in considering this spiritual work of mercy as a work of charity at all. All the works of mercy have reference to our neighbor. They are variations of the command to do alms, whether corporal or spiritual. To bear wrongs would seem to be a passive rather than an active virtue; to concern one's self solely, rather than one's neighbor. But when you look at it closely, you find that it does concern others rather than yourself; that it is not merely the endurance of ills which may just happen, or which may be called "Acts of God," but the endurance of wrongs which come to us from our neighbor. Why then is it an act of charity or mercy or alms to him, for me to bear the wrongs which he inflicts on me? It is not merely a food to my own patience and humility. It must be a benefit to *him;* otherwise it would not be an act of charity to my neighbor. The whole matter is explained by St. Paul. In the Epistle to the Romans (12:14–21) he writes: "Bless those who persecute you; bless and do not curse. Rejoice with those who rejoice; weep with those who weep. Be of one mind toward one another. . . . To no man render evil for evil, but provide good things, not only in the sight of God, but also in the sight of all men. If it be possible, as far as in you lies, be at peace with all men. Do not avenge yourselves, beloved; but give place to the wrath, for it is written, *Revenge is mine, I will repay,* says the Lord. *But if thy enemy is hungry, give him food; if he*

is thirsty, give him drink. For by so doing this thou wilt heap coals of fire upon his head. Be not overcome by evil, but overcome evil with good." The words italicized are quoted by St. Paul from Proverbs (25:21f.).

It is the command in plain words, "to take it on the chin," and say nothing about it, so as to remain at peace with your neighbor.

It is the command of our Lord in the Sermon on the Mount: "But I say to you not to resist the evil doer; on the contrary, if someone strike thee on the right cheek, turn to him the other also" (Matt. 5:39). It is the duty of being silent under attack from another, so as to spare him; to use no recriminations that would anger him the more, and thus save him from committing greater sin. It is primarily a concern for his salvation. Someone has said that silence is the most crushing repartee. But generally that is a scornful silence, and more antagonistic than a blast of words. The more Christian approach is the soft answer that turns away wrath. The silent endurance taught by the Gospel is animated by the spirit of charity, by a love for neighbor. The Book of Proverbs (15:1) has the gist of it: "A mild answer breaketh wrath; but a harsh word stirreth up fury." That theme of the mild answer is common enough in the Old Testament. Ecclesiasticus (19:10) says: "Hast thou heard a word against thy neighbor: let it die within thee, trusting that it will not burst thee." "My son, in thy good deeds make no complaint, and when thou givest anything add not grief by an evil word. Shall not the dew assuage the heat?" (Ecclus. 18:15–16.) There it is again — spare your neighbor, don't get back at him, pour oil on the troubled waters, return good for evil. It is not easy doctrine. In our pride we rebel against attacks. We all want to have the last word. Judith (8:26–27) exhorted the ancients of her people: "Let us not revenge ourselves for these things which we suffer. But esteeming these very punishments to be less than our sins deserve, let us believe that these scourges of the Lord, with which like servants we are chastised, have happened for our amendment, and not for our destruction."

But it is our Lord who asks us to "be glad and rejoice" when we suffer for His sake, "for your reward is very great in heaven" (Matt. 5:12). And in a more general way He bids us: "Pray for them that persecute and calumniate you" (Matt. 5:44).

Our Lord was the Great Exemplar of endurance. He was led as a sheep to the slaughter, and did not open His mouth to reproach. The Apostles imitated Him. They were reviled, but they did not revile in return. St. Paul even rejoiced in his tribulations: "I rejoice now in the sufferings I bear for your sake; and what is lacking of the sufferings of Christ I fill up in my flesh for his body, which is the Church" (Col. 1:24). And so he urges on his flock: "Let all bitterness, and wrath, and indignation and clamor, and reviling be removed from you, along with all malice. On the contrary, be kind to one another and merciful, generously forgiving one another as also God in Christ has generously forgiven you" (Eph. 4:32). And finally he says: "If we endure, we shall also reign with him" (2 Tim. 2:13).

Patience, patience, patience; that is the message of all the Apostles as it was the message of Christ, and, be it understood, a patience that was not only for the strengthening of one's own soul, but for the calming and converting of the soul of one's neighbor.

Now, so much insistence is put upon this because, of all the works of mercy, it is the hardest to perform. It is easy enough to give money, food, a cup of water; easy enough to correct others. But to refrain from the petty revenge of getting square, and to be willing to turn the other cheek is a pretty difficult assignment. We all have the gift of the tongue, only we do not make the gift as an alms. We usually slash about with it as a two-edged sword.

But hard as the task is, it is of the very essence of Christianity. To be a true follower of Christ we must bite our tongue. Not that we are obliged to stand every abuse from our neighbor. It would be heroic to do so in some cases; but there are circumstances where, for reasons other than personal, we are obliged in duty to defend ourselves from calumniating slurs, but this, too, for the sake of our neighbor, so as not to scandalize him. Our Lord gave the example of that. He was patient under opposition, bitter hatred, personal physical pain. But when His enemies accused Him of being posesssed by the devil, He repelled the calumny with all His might. The reason was because that horrible charge, if not repulsed, would have destroyed the efficacy of His Divine mission.

The saints, too, distinguished between attacks upon them as private individuals and attacks upon their official position. St. Paul preached patience, long-suffering, and endured every persecution so long as it affected only him, but he resented any slur upon his importance as an Apostle. He would let no one poison the wells. But apart from that distinction of the personal and the official, the saints, as in all things else, are models of keeping the peace by turning the other cheek.

One day the brethren of St. Anthony of the Desert asked him the secret of salvation. He replied: "Have you not heard that Jesus said, "If one strike thee on thy right cheek, turn to him also the other?" "Yes," said the brothers, "but that is beyond our strength." St. Anthony replied: "Then at least suffer in patience when you are struck on one cheek." Still they demurred: "That is still beyond our strength." "Well," continued Anthony, "be content not to strike back when you have been struck." Again they replied: "But even that is beyond our strength." Anthony was evidently disgusted. He turned to one of his followers and said, "Go and make a fortifying drink for these brethren, for in truth they are very feeble.

And, as for you, brethren, prayer is the only thing I can recommend to you."

St. Peter Martyr was the object of unjust accusation, but he bore it all patiently, even though he was forbidden to preach. He was finally exonerated.

The devil said to St. Macarius: "I can surpass you in vigils, in fasting, and in many other things, but humility conquers and disarms me." Once a young man asked Macarius for spiritual advice. Macarius told him to go to a certain graveyard and reproach the dead, and then flatter them. He did so, and went back and told Macarius that whether he reproached or flattered, the dead refused to answer. "Then," said Macarius, "learn to be moved neither by injuries nor by flatteries. If you die to the world and to yourself, you will begin to live to Christ."

When St. Fulgentius was so persecuted by the Arians that even some of the Arians were ashamed, their bishop promised to punish them if Fulgentius said the word, but he replied, "A Christian is never allowed to seek revenge," and he went on to say that as for himself it was incumbent upon him not to lose the advantages of patience and forgiveness of injuries. That was a manly attitude, and a Christian was first of all a real man. Pancratius was a boy of fourteen, but when the Emperor tried to break him down by telling him that he was "only a child," the young martyr replied: "In body I am a child, but I have a man's heart." How that answer would have delighted St. Catherine who preached to everybody: "Be manly!"

One night at supper St. Benedict was being served by a monk who was the son of a senator. The young monk said to himself: "Who is this man that I should serve at his table and hold the light for him." St. Benedict read the monk's heart, but he did not flare up in protest against his pride. He gave the soft answer, and calmly said, "Sound your heart, son, sound your heart." St. Bernard said that there were three kinds of patience: to bear insulting words, to bear damage to one's goods, and to bear bodily injuries. Once he wrote to a bishop and gave him friendly advice. But the bishop became angry, and replied: "Health to thee, and not to thy spirit of blasphemy." Bernard felt obliged, for the cause, not for himself to refute that. "I do not believe," he said, "that I have the spirit of blasphemy, nor that I have spoken irreverently to anyone, nor wished so to speak, especially to a prince among my people."

When St. Francis, at the beginning of the movement, was sending out his six disciples, he said to them: "Be patient in trouble, give to all who insult you a humble answer, bless those who persecute you, thank those who do you wrong and slander you, because for all this your reward shall be great in heaven. . . . You will find some men who are true, good and peaceful; they will receive you and your word with gladness. Others, and these in great number, you will on the other hand find to be revilers of God; they will oppose you and speak against you. Be prepared, therefore, to endure all things patiently."

Francis soon had need to be patient. He was treated as a poor fool, pelted with dirt, robbed of his clothes, but he kept turning the other cheek, and soon won many by this spiritual alms. He took it all in stride. He said that if the friars cast up to him: "You dislike us for you are unlettered, slow of speech, a fool, a simpleton (and this I am, cast out with reviling, little esteemed of all) I tell you, unless I can hear such words with unchanged gladness of spirit, and unchanged holy intent, I am vainly called Brother Minor." All these shameful reproaches he endured for the Cross of Christ, and to win his neighbor to God. There is a famous sermon he made to Brother Leo. He said that if the friars gave the example of holiness and edification all over the world, they would not find perfect happiness in that; if they cured the blind and lame and dumb, and cast out devils and even raised to life those who had been dead four days, they would not find perfect happiness in that; if they spoke all tongues and knew all wisdom and all the Scriptures, and were able to reveal the secrets of hearts; if they spoke with tongues of angels, and knew the courses of the stars and the powers of herbs, and could preach so as to convert the infidels, not even then would they have perfect happiness. But if they came to the Portiuncula wet and frozen and dirty, and were refused admittance as robbers, and then stood there and endured it all without complaint, and even thought that the porter knew them as they really were — then, said he, they would have perfect happiness.

He practised what he preached. He would ask one of the friars to say insulting words to him, and he would rejoice at it. "The Lord bless you, dearest son," he would say, "for you have spoken words most true and such as it becomes the son of Peter Bernardone to hear."

Among all the saints nobody bore wrongs patiently out of love for neighbor better than St. Catherine of Siena. We have spoken much of her in this book and of St. Francis and St. Teresa. Other saints might have been referred to at length but these three were especial Apostles of love, and stand out as beacon lights in the works of mercy.

When St. Catherine refused to marry, all her family persecuted her, refused to speak to her, made her do all the housework, practically kept her a prisoner, in the effort to break her spirit, but she returned their recriminations with love and practical charity. Her life, especially during her last days, was one of suffering, which she gladly endured. An oft-repeated expression of hers was "Endure"; and she continually preached this endurance to others. When she was vilified because she did not eat or drink when she was physically unable to do so she bore the abuse without complaint. She said to somone: "If in future anyone speaks evil of me, then you must only answer them that a great deal more might be said, and they do not say nearly enough." But some things she would not endure, lest scandal be given to her neighbor. When she was accused of too much familiarity with priests, she defended her reputation. "By the grace of God," she declared, "I am a virgin!" She would stand no accusation that would undermine her work for God. "Alas, Lord," she said, "if only I could believe that I suffered unjustly, that I suffered with Thee, I ask for nothing else." She welcomed persecution, but she could also write: "I beg you not to be light in judging, if you are not clearly illumined by God." Our Lord said to her, "A man proves his patience on his neighbor when he receives injury from him."

"Manly endurance with patience" was what our Lord demanded of her; and she begged others from the pope down to have this manliness.

It is told of St. Lydwine, the famous mystic, that once a crowd of soldiers stripped her, called her a bad woman, but she patiently bore all the horrible indignities, and even prayed for those who had insulted her.

To come back again to St. Teresa. — Her motto was, "To Die or to Suffer." For forty years she was not without pain. "Our Lord," she said, "does not seem to wish me to be long without suffering." It was not only physical pain, it was the worse one, of calumny. She once wrote from Seville: "The injustices, the falsehoods, and the duplicity one meets with here are astonishing. — In the midst of all these troubles I have felt an extraordinary joy." Again: "Should the fault be laid on me, it will not be the first time. I have been blamed when innocent, but experience has taught me that when our Lord is pleased, He smoothes the way." Her opponents, the Mitigated Carmelites, were even planning to get rid of her by sending her to the Indies; there were calumnies about her and Father Gracian; when she was elected Prioress of the

Incarnation Convent, at Ávila, the new Provincial excommunicated the fifty-five nuns who had voted for her and persecuted them for three months; even their confessor, the great St. John of the Cross, was imprisoned and treated inhumanly; but she made it her maxim: "Receive reprimands with interior and outward humility, and pray for your admonisher." She bore, but she would not demean herself. When she was charged by the Rector of the Jesuits at Ávila with abetting a certain Jesuit and trying to induce him to leave the Society for another order, she retorted: "I have spoken to you with perfect sincerity and I believe I have done all that is required by self-respect and Christianity."

But, much as she was maligned, she never regarded herself as a martyr. She had too fine a sense of humor for that. She could laugh it off. "As to the evil speaking directed against me," she wrote, "which is considerable and highly injurious to me, and done by many, I find myself herein also very much the better. I think that what they say makes scarcely any more impression upon me than it would upon an idiot."

Just there lies the secret of bearing wrongs patiently — to be willing to be a fool for the sake of Christ. The fool is never allowed to take himself seriously. The office of the "King's Fool," or court jester, was to amuse the king and his courtiers. Often the fool was wiser than the people he made laugh — as witness the jesters of Shakespeare. It would be wise for everyone of us to be in this respect like the idiot referred to by St. Teresa — to be a fool for love. When your adversary sees that in spite of his hate, his desire to hurt you, his glee in causing you harm, you do not slash back at him but are kind and forgiving, that you give love for hate, he may, by the grace of God get the wisdom to see what a fool he is to damn his soul for a petty grievance; and so your forbearance may win him back to God. Your mercy may win him God's mercy.

The real strength of the soul is in meekness. So we pray, "Jesus, meek and humble of heart, make my heart like to Thine." To give the meek answer for the purpose of bringing our neighbor back to God is Christian heroism at its best.

Mother of Mercy, Queen of Sorrow, pray for us!

Chapter XVII

To Forgive All Injuries

THERE is something wonderfully noble about a forgiving man. He is a big man, a "manly man." Cicero said in praise of Caesar: "None of your virtues is more admirable and gracious than your mercy." It is not only human, it is Divine.

> To err is human, to forgive Divine.

Our God is the God of mercy. We know He is Infinite Justice, and we do not minimize that divine attribute. God is not mocked. But we are not to blame if we prefer to think of Him as Infinite Mercy. He began it. We are taught by Him to plead over and over, "Lord, have mercy!" Who ever prays for justice? It is always for mercy, for forgiveness. What a horrible end we face if God will not show us mercy!

The whole theory of mercy is worked out so logically. Here it is: Since you expect mercy, you must show mercy. Shakespeare has Portia express it thus:

> Consider this,
> That, in the course of justice, none of us
> Should see salvation: we do pray for mercy;
> And the same prayer doth teach us all to render
> The deeds of mercy.

Merely a reference to the Lord's prayer, but with the old traditional Catholic homiletics which he must have heard many times.

When we pray for mercy, generally speaking that mercy has reference not to alms for corporal needs, but to forgiveness of sin. Mercy is, indeed, a broad term — as we have seen, "alms" means mercy — and it includes all the corporal and spiritual works of charity to our neighbor. Hence while many of the Scriptural references to "mercy" are rightly interpreted as meaning corporal alms specifically, there are many instances where mercy must refer to forgiveness. Indeed, the whole of the Old Testament is the development of the promise of a Redeemer, of Him who will come to atone for the sin of Adam and bring forgiveness. "Mercy!" is the ceaseless cry of the penitent David. Other than David's pleas for forgiveness, and the fundamental promise of an atoning and forgiving Messias, there are few, if any, references in the Old Testament to the forgiveness of injuries done by one's neighbor, a fact which, as we shall see, our Lord makes much of.

The Old Testament is a call to repentance before the face of God, and the assurance of mercy to the penitent; "for the Highest hateth sinners, and hath mercy on the penitent" (Ecclus. 12:3).

But the New Testament, being the fulfillment of the promise of God's forgiveness, is forever appealing to man to forgive his neighbor, and laying that down as a necessary condition in order to obtain the forgiveness of God. Almost the first words of our Lord at the beginning of His mission are, "Blessed are the merciful," "Love your enemies"; and almost His last words were, "Father, forgive them for they know not what they do." So important is the command to forgive our enemies, and even love them, that He goes into it with more detail than in any other of His teachings. Thus He says: "Love your enemies, do good to those who hate you. Bless those who curse you, pray for those who calumniate you. And to him who strikes thee on the one cheek, offer the other also; and from him who takes away thy cloak, do not withhold thy tunic also. Give to everyone who asks of thee, and from him who takes away thy goods, ask no return. And even as you wish men to do to you, so also do you to others. And if you love those who love you, what merit have you? For even sinners love those who love them. And if you do good to those who do good to you, what merit have you? For even sinners do that. And if you lend to those from whom you hope to receive in return, what merit have you? For even sinners lend to sinners, that they may get back as much in return. But love your enemies; and do good, and lend" (Luke 6:27 ff.). "Do not judge, and you shall not be judged; do not condemn and you shall not be condemned. Forgive, and you shall be forgiven. . . . With what measure you measure, it shall be measured to you (*Ibid.* 6:37–38). "But why dost thou see the speck in thy brother's eye, and yet dost not consider the beam in thine own eye?" (*Ibid.* 7:41.) "If thy brother sin, rebuke him; and if he repent, forgive him. And if seven times in the day he sin against thee, and seven times in the day turn back to thee, saying 'I repent,' forgive him" (*Ibid.* 17:3–4).

Tremendous teaching. But our Lord went further than that. One day Peter said to Him: "Lord, how often shall my brother sin against me, and I forgive him?" Our Lord answered: "I do not say to thee seven times, but seventy times seven." That means, of course, indefinitely. Thereupon, He gave the parable about the unmerciful servant who had been forgiven by his master a debt of ten thousand talents, an incredible sum, but who in turn refused to forgive a petty debt to a fellow servant. The master, outraged at such ingratitude, delivered the merciless servant to the torturers until he would pay the debt; he never would be able to pay such a debt. Our Lord drew the terrible conclusion: "So also shall my heavenly Father do to you, if you forgive not everyone his brother from your hearts" (Matt. 18:35).

Again He said: "You have heard that it was said to the ancients, 'Thou shalt not kill,' and that whoever shall murder shall be liable to judgment, but I say to you that everyone who is angry with his brother shall be liable to judgment, and whoever says to his brother 'Raca' [i.e., empty-headed], shall be liable to the Sanhedrin, and whoever says, 'Thou Fool!' shall be liable to the fire of Gehenna. Therefore, if thou art offering thy gift at the altar, and there thou rememberest that thy brother has anything against thee, leave thy gift before the altar, and go first to be reconciled to thy brother, and then come and offer thy gift. Come to terms with thy opponent quickly while thou art with him on the way; lest thy opponent deliver thee to the judge, and the judge to the officer, and thou be cast into prison. Amen I say to thee, thou wilt not come out from it until thou hast paid the last penny" (Matt. 5:21–26).

Rather a long quotation, and even more of like import could be given; but the teaching is so fundamental, and in our Lord's own words, that a treatise on forgiveness, though filled with sayings and doings of the saints, would be quite empty without it.

And here is the climax. When our Lord made *the* prayer for His disciples — the *Our Father* — it contained, as a summary, all His teaching about forgiveness — "Forgive us our debts as we also forgive our debtors." And here is the sanction: *"For if you forgive men their offences, your Heavenly Father will also forgive you your offences. But if you do not forgive men, neither will your Father forgive you your offences"* (Matt. 6:14–15).

Hence it is clear that our Lord put the strongest insistence on the forgiveness of injuries. It was vital to His Kingdom, which must be one of peace and brotherly love. The Apostles repeated that fundamental teaching. "Bear with one another and forgive one another," says St. Paul; "if anyone has a grievance against any other; even as the

Lord has forgiven you, so also do you forgive" (Col. 3:13).
"But if you bite and devour one another, take heed or
you will be consumed by one another" (Gal. 5:15).

St. John, the Apostle of Love, has strong words about
hate: "He who . . . hates his brother is in the darkness,
and walks in the darkness" (1 John 2:9). "If anyone says,
'I love God,' and hates his neighbor, he is a liar" (1 John
4:19–20).

When St. John the Almoner was thanked by a man for
generous alms, he said, "Brother I have not yet spilt my
blood for you, as Jesus Christ, my Master, and my God
commands me." And that is the theme of all the saints
in regard to this work of mercy; if Christ, to obtain my
salvation has died for me, I must, if I am to imitate Him,
set no limit to my forgiveness of injuries done me by my
brother in Christ. The importance of this Christian teaching is evident. If hate were permitted to have full sway,
there would soon be an end to all civilization. Peace and
love are necessary for the very continuance of the world.
God knows, we have seen enough in our own day of the
horrible destruction of war. It shows why our Lord spoke
at such length on the absolute need of eliminating from
earth that pride and hate which seek to nullify His work.

The spirit of the saints is the spirit of forgiveness. God
had forgiven them so much, the least they could do was
to forgive their neighbor. They would imitate Christ. As
St. Cyprian said, "We must endeavor to imitate the patience of God." St. Augustine had been a great sinner;
he became a great pardoner. Said he: "God shows mercy
to us on account of His goodness, but we, in turn, show
mercy to one another on account of Him; that is, He
has compassion on us that we may enjoy Himself; but we
show compassion to one another in order that we may
enjoy Him." Again: "That men might become the children of God, God condescended to become the child of
man. Ah! then, who any longer will be able to cherish

any hatred against man, whose nature and resemblance he finds in the humanity of God? *To hate him would be to hate God."*

St. Caesarius of Arles (470–543) said a very striking thing: "As for other good works, there may perhaps be found an excuse where they are not practised; but there is no excuse where charity is wanting. Some one may say, 'I cannot fast,' but who can say, 'I cannot love'? One may say, 'Because of the weakness of my body I cannot abstain from meat'; but who can say, 'I cannot love my enemies or pardon those who have offended me' "? When the populace tore down a statue of the Emperor Theodosius and his family, the emperor determined to take vengeance. Bishop Flavian interceded. "Your clemency on this occasion," he said, "will be more honorable to you than your most celebrated victories." The emperor replied: "If Jesus Christ, the Lord of all things, vouchsafed to pardon and pray for those very men who crucified Him, ought I to hesitate to pardon them who have offended me?"

St. Remigius, or Remi, the great apostle of the French, had foreseen a famine and had stored up corn to meet it. He was ridiculed. A mob set fire to the granary, and when the old bishop arrived on the scene, everything had been burned to the ground. He got off his horse, and with no condemnation of the criminals, simply said: "A hearth is always good, especially for an old man." St. Hugh (1132) often cast himself at the feet of others and begged them to pardon injuries or to make some necessary satisfaction to their neighbors. The story of St. John Gualbert is often told. His brother Hugh had been murdered, and John determined to avenge his death. He met the murderer on a narrow bridge. It was Good Friday. The murderer begged for mercy by the Passion of Jesus Christ, and John spared his life. He went to a near-by monastery to pray, and there, while he was kneeling before a crucifix the head of Christ bowed to him, in reward for the mercy he had shown. John entered the monastery to become a monk. He died a saint — because he had forgiven his neighbor.

In the days of St. Francis of Assisi there were continual wars, especially between Assisi and Perugia. He often denounced the spirit of hatred which kept his community in perpetual turmoil. Once he met a poor man who was very bitter against his master. Francis said to him: "I will willingly give you my hood if you will forgive your master his injustice." The man, perhaps for the sake of the bribe, agreed to pardon the offender. It was a cheap victory for Francis, who would part with any possession in order to bring peace to a soul. He was, like his Divine Master, a worker for peace. If one of his friars by a hasty word hurt another's feelings, he would not rest till he had restored peace between them. "As sure as you love the Lord and me," he said, "see to it that no brother in the whole world, let him have sinned as he may, in any way is permitted to go from you without forgiveness. And if he comes even a thousand times before your eyes with sin, then love him altogether more than you love me, that you may draw him to the Lord, and be always merciful to such."

Just there is the secret of the obligation of forgiveness, not only to get rancor out of your own heart, since love and hate cannot dwell together, but also to draw your neighbor who has offended you to the Lord, and induce him to get the sin of hatred out of his heart. Being an alms, it is a gift you make him for his spiritual benefit, and for yourself, too.

It blesses him that gives and him that takes.

An old writer, Guy de Roye, once said: "God has given you eyes in order that you might look on others with pity." St. Bonaventure said to his friars: "All men are your friends, and no one is to be called an enemy; for they who are angry with you, and who persecute you, confer the greatest benefit on your souls, more than you

could receive from the sweetest friend. All men, therefore, confer favors on you; and, besides yourselves, you
can have no enemy." St. Bernard wrote to a friend: "You
are too bitter against this man. I fear that your zeal is
not according to knowledge." St. Vincent of Beauvais said,
"A prince who would know all things must pardon many."

St. Francis de Sales is unusually strong in discussing this
matter of forgiveness. He says: "He that is given to fasting
holds himself as very devout, if he do but fast, though his
heart be full of rancor; and though he dare not moisten
his tongue in wine or even in water for fear of trans-
gressing sobriety, yet he scruples not to plunge it in the
blood of his neighbor, by detraction and calumny."

Again he says: "Another will readily draw an alms out
of his purse to give it to the poor, but he cannot draw
any gentleness out of his heart to forgive his enemies."

St. Teresa saw the deep spirituality in forgiveness of
injuries. She wrote: "To insure that persecutions and in-
sults should bear good fruit and profit the soul, it is well
to consider that they are done to God before they are
done to me, for the blow aimed at me has already been
aimed at His Majesty by sin." Once she wrote this to the
nuns: "I often tell you, sisters, and now I leave it to you
in writing, that not only those dwelling in this house but
all who aspire after perfection must fly a thousand leagues
away from saying, 'I was *right;* it was not *right* for me to
suffer this, they had no *right* to do such a thing to me!'
Now God deliver us from such wrong rights!"

"Do not suppose that one who suffers does not pray,"
she said. That was her motto, even to the end. Shortly
before her death she left Valladolid with the intention of
going to Ávila. Blessed Anne of St. Bartholomew, her
companion, relates that the Prioress, Mother Mary Baptist — Teresa's old friend — ordered them to leave the convent. "Go away, both of you," she said, "and never come
back." The nuns of Medina also received her unkindly.

She reached Alba in a dying condition, and passed away, October 4, the feast of St. Francis, another preacher of the works of mercy.

Silvio Pellico, treated so inhumanly as a prisoner, wrote in his famous book, "My Prisons": "When I could again pray sincerely for all the world and abandon all hatred, my doubts as to faith vanished." There is a close connection between faith and love.

One of the great works that Father Olier, the founder of the Sulpicians, did was to put an end to dueling in the Paris of his day. It was a crying evil in the parish of St. Sulpice. Seventeen men were killed in duels in one week. Olier made the nobles promise not to engage in dueling. His was an heroic act of mercy.

Daniel O'Connell was a great man, but he never was as great a Catholic as when he refused to fight a duel.

The famous Benedictine writer, Louis de Blois, sums up all the teaching about this spiritual work of mercy as follows: "If when any difference has given rise to bitterness between you and your brethren, you do not seek to be reconciled to him, if you do not forget the injury he has done to you, but, on the contrary, if you cherish a secret resentment or a less sincere affection for him, you are not a servant of Jesus Christ, you are not a Christian, you are abominable before God."

Sometimes we think we are asked to do a lot when we are asked to forgive our neighbor. Our heart is torn, our pride is pierced, our mind is in a turmoil from cruel words, unkind sneers or slurs. It *is* hard to forgive a false friend, especially one that shows no desire to help in picking up the broken pieces; but, hard as it is, there is no other way out. God has demanded our surrender, by saying to us — "If you do not forgive him, I will not forgive you!" What a tragedy if, for petty spite, we seal our own condemnation.

"O Mother of God, and Mother of Mercy, pray for us and for all!

Chapter XVIII

To Pray for the Living and the Dead

PRAYER is the theme that runs all through the Scriptures, both the Old Testament and the New. The Psalms, for example, are a prayer book, from the first word to the last. Our Lord was always insisting on prayer, pray always, pray without ceasing. He taught His disciples how to pray by creating for them the *Our Father*. There were prayers of every kind, prayers of adoration, prayers for mercy, prayers for material bread as well as spiritual, prayers of thanksgiving. But our field here is limited. We are not writing a general treatise on prayer, but are limiting our discussion to that special prayer with which the spiritual work of mercy is concerned, the prayer not for ourselves — though, indeed, every prayer to God is necessarily a prayer for ourselves — but the prayer for the living and the dead.

From the beginning of God's dealings with man, there is recognized the duty as well as the usefulness of praying for one's neighbor. When Abimelech, under a misapprehension, had attempted to take Abraham's wife Sara, God said to him, "Restore the man his wife, for he is a prophet: and he shall pray for thee, and thou shalt live" (Gen. 20:7). Samuel said to the people, "Gather all Israel to Masphath, that I may pray to the Lord for you" (1 Kings 7:5). Even the pagan King Darius recognized the efficacy of prayer.

When he had restored the exiled Jews to their country, he sent this message to them: "Let them offer oblations to the God of Heaven, and pray for the life of the king and his children" (1 Esd. 6:10). God said to Job's useless comforters: "My servant Job shall pray for you" (Job 42:8). King Sedecias, another pagan, sent messengers to say to Jeremias: "Pray to the Lord our God for us" (Jer. 37:3).

But our Lord, of course, is the authority on prayer. His command was, to pray even for "them that persecute and calumniate you" (Matt. 5:44). It is sublimely expressed in the *"Our Father."* Note the *"Our"*; give *us* this day *our* daily bread; forgive *us;* lead *us* not into temptation; deliver *us* — all those phrases are interpreted as implying a prayer not only for ourselves but for our neighbor. This exchange of prayer, or communion of prayer, is evident in the very first days of the Church. Even Simon the Magician begs Peter: "Do you pray for me to the Lord" (Acts 8:24). St. Paul never ceases to pray for his converts: "We pray God that you may do no evil" (2 Cor. 13:7); "we, too, have been praying for you unceasingly" (Col. 1:9). And at the same time he begs their prayers: "Brethren, pray for us" (1 Thess. 5:25). Then there is the famous passage from St. James in reference to prayers for the sick: "Is any one among you sick? Let him bring in the presbyters of the Church, and let them pray over him" (5:13).

The prayers, both for the living and the dead, have a very prominent place in the early liturgies. There is one prayer particularly that we must quote from the Liturgy according to St. James. It is a trifle long, but since the Liturgy is not readily available to everybody, it would be a pity to omit it, since historically it gives a fine picture of the early Church at work, and is also a splendid argument for the Communion of Saints as practised by the first believers.

Save us, have mercy on us, pity and keep us, O God, by Thy grace.

For the peace that is from above, and the loving-kindness of God, and the salvation of our souls, let us beseech the Lord.

For the peace of the whole world, and the unity of all the holy churches of God, let us beseech the Lord.

For those who bear fruit, and labor honorably in the holy churches of God; for those who remember the poor, the widows and the orphans, the strangers and needy ones; and for those who have requested us to mention them in our prayers, let us beseech the Lord.

For those who are in old age and infirmity, for the sick and suffering, and those who are troubled by unclean spirits, for their speedy cure from God and their salvation, let us beseech the Lord.

For those who are passing their days in virginity, and celibacy, and discipline, and for those in holy matrimony; and for the holy fathers and brethren agonizing in mountains, and dens, and caves of the earth, let us beseech the Lord.

For Christians sailing, traveling, living among strangers, and for our brethren in captivity, in exile, in prison, and in bitter slavery, their peaceful return, let us beseech the Lord.

For the remission of our sins, and forgiveness of our transgressions, and for our deliverance from all tribulation, wrath, danger, and constraint, and uprising of enemies against us, let us beseech the Lord.

For favorable weather, peaceful showers, beneficent dews, abundance of fruits, the perfect close of a good season, and for the crown of the year, let us beseech the Lord.

For our fathers and brethren present, and praying with us in this holy hour, and at every season, their zeal, labor and earnestness, let us beseech the Lord.

For every Christian soul in tribulation and distress, and needing the mercy and succor of God; for the return of the erring, the health of the sick, the deliverance of the captives, the rest of the fathers that have fallen asleep aforetime, let us beseech the Lord.

For the hearing and acceptance of our prayer before God, and the sending down on us His rich mercies and compassion, let us beseech the Lord.

Let us commemorate our all-holy, pure, most glorious blessed Lady, God's mother, and ever-virgin Mary, and all the holy and just, that we may all find mercy through their prayers and intercessions.

And for the offered, precious, heavenly, unutterable, pure, glorious, dread, awful, divine gifts, and the salvation of the priest who stands by and offers them, let us offer supplication to God the Lord.

This glorious prayer, so like our own prayers today, is the epitome of the history of the first Christians. It is, as we have said, a commentary on the Communion of Saints, a vital teaching so loved from the beginning. Tertullian speaks of the Christians as having "common hope, fear, joy, sorrow, and suffering"; and St. Augustine speaks of "the unity of charity." That, in a word, is the meaning of the Communion of Saints, that between the members of the Church, in heaven, purgatory, and on earth — according to the words of the Catechism of Trent — "there exists, by reason of their close union with one another under Christ their Head, a mutual communication in spiritual riches."

We, Christ's children, living or dead, are all one family, and the members of the Church, in heaven, on earth, and in purgatory are in communion with one another, as being one body in Jesus Christ. That the faithful on earth can assist one another is the teaching, as we have seen, both in the Old and the New Testament. But it is especially evident in the practice of the Church. In the Mass the Church is constantly praying for the living members. And the practice of all the religious societies, of all Catholic individuals, indeed, is to pray for the living. "Pray for me," is our constant appeal to others.

The Emperor Valens asked a noble Persian, who had become a monk, "Where are you going?" The monk replied, "I go to pray for your Empire."

So it has been said that "the first of all the services which the monks have conferred upon Christian society was that of praying, of praying much, of praying always for those whose prayers were evil or who prayed not at all."

And the Catholic people relied much upon the prayers of the monks. When Philip Augustus was sailing with his fleet to the Holy Land, a severe tempest arose. But he was not afraid. "It is midnight," he said, "it is the hour when the Community at Clairvaux arise to sing Matins. These holy monks never forget us, they are going to appease Christ, they go to pray for us; and their prayers will deliver us out of peril."

It was a Swedish monk who said: "More is done for the world by those who pray than by those who fight." As King Arthur says in Tennyson's *Idylls of the King,* "More things are wrought by prayer than this world dreams of." St. Teresa said to her own sister: "I ask you one thing as a charity, not to love me because I look after your worldly interests, but because I pray for you." It is told of her that she showed her constant charity for her neighbor in many ways, chiefly by her ardent desire for the salvation of souls. She often wept over the darkness of infidels and heretics, not only continually praying God to enlighten them, but offering for them fasts, disciplines, and other bodily mortifications. She made a resolution, and kept it, not to let a day pass without doing an act of charity. It was like the charity of her namesake, the Little Flower, who tells us that her chief motive in entering Carmel was to pray for priests. There is an especially lovely Community, the "Sisters of the Little Company of Mary," who bind themselves to pray day and night for the sick and dying. Attached to the Community is a Confraternity, called the "Confraternity of Calvary," the members of which assist by prayer those who are in their last agony, and also, if possible, by personal attendance.

The Church has always cultivated the family spirit. We all are members, children, of her one big family. The least we can do is pray for one another.

As to praying for the dead, that is one of the tenderest

things about the Church. She is a mother who never forgets. And, like all mothers, she is most loving and most tender to her suffering children. We are not concerned here with proving the existence of purgatory. Enough, that it has been the practice of the Church from the beginning to pray for the dead and to encourage her children to do so. It would take too much space to note the passages from the Fathers; such texts as that of St. John Chrysostom, that we should assist the dead, "not with lamentations, but with prayers, supplications and alms." Note the "alms" as a means to help the poor souls.

In the Liturgy of St. James, just as in our Mass today, we find the Commemoration of the dead: "Remember, O Lord God, the spirits of all flesh, of whom we have made mention, and of whom we have not made mention, who are of the true faith, from righteous Abel unto this day; unto them do Thou give rest there in the land of the living, in Thy Kingdom, in the joy of Paradise, in the bosom of Abraham, and of Isaac, and of Jacob, our holy fathers; whence pain, and grief and lamentations have fled: there the light of Thy countenance looks upon them, and enlightens them forever."

The desire to be buried with the martyrs, and the general custom that prevailed in the catacombs of laying one's loved ones close to these saints, showed how eager the first Christians were to help the dead. The erection of monuments and the engraving on slabs was not so much to preserve the name of the departed, as to call attention to his need and to beg prayers for him.

It has been well said that the Church is one big Purgatorial Society. She has never failed to try to get as many prayers as she could for her dead children. She is ever seeking new ways to help them. It would be quite impossible to count the indulgences she grants in favor of them. Her continual prayer is for them. Not only are there special Masses for the dead — the Mass on the day of decease or burial, the Mass on the third day, the seventh, the thirtieth, the anniversary, the daily — but she concludes almost every prayer with entreaty for the souls of the faithful departed to rest in peace. The Living God is always among the dead, eager to bring them to eternal life.

In the monasteries, particularly, there was that ceaseless prayer for the poor souls. It was, for instance, the Order of Cluny that first practised the Commemoration of All Souls' Day. The religious confraternities that arose for this purpose are innumerable. That was one of the prime purposes of the Medieval Guilds, to pray for the dead, so that it can be truthfully said that everyone in the Middle Ages belonged to some kind of Purgatorial Society.

One of the many crimes of the Reformation in England was the destruction of more than twenty-three Chantries. The Chantry, besides being a school for the poor, was an endowment of one or several priests to say Mass daily for the soul of the endower and his intentions. So universal was the custom to remember the souls of the departed, that chapels were built on battlefields and endowed, so as to assure continual Masses and prayers for the deceased soldiers.

Always the Church has a great treasury of Masses, prayers, alms, indulgences for the souls in Purgatory. So the Church is always urging us to do this spiritual work of mercy, to pray for the living and the dead. To spend money on material alms may mean sacrifice. To breathe a prayer will cost us little effort. How, then, can we hope for God's mercy to us if we refuse to do that easiest of alms, a prayer of mercy for our living and dead brothers in Christ.

So ends our consideration of the works of mercy. May it be with the determination to devote ourselves to the practice of them, a practice that entails so little labor in doing, but brings with it heavenly rewards. They are the crown of our faith, the testimony of our love.

Frederick Ozanam, when only twenty, and his young companions, "eight poor fellows," were taunted by their non-Catholic friends. "Yes," said they, "you have a right to speak of the past. In bygone days Christianity did indeed work wonders, but today Christianity is dead. And you, who boast of being Catholics, what do you do? What works can you show which prove your faith, and can claim to make us respect and acknowledge it?"

Yes; what works can you show? The answer of Ozanam and his companions was the foundation of the great Society of St. Vincent de Paul, which has transformed the modern world. Ozanam's aim in founding the Society was, as he says, "to insure my faith by works of charity."

"To insure my faith!" There is our motto in doing the works of mercy. Love to increase our faith, and love and faith to lead us through the door of our neighbor's house to the full fruition of our hope in Him who said: "Come, blessed of my Father . . . as long as you did it for one of these, the least of my brethren, you did it for me."

Mary, Mother of Mercy, you "who have died in the embrace of the Lord," pray for us!